748.2
Wea
c.2

Weatherman, Hazel
        Colored glass-
    ware of the depress-
    ion era

10.00

SEP 10 1984 *Grace Wood*

Colored Glassware of the Depression Era

Colored Glassware

of the

Depression Era

Hazel Marie Weatherman

Additional copies of Hazel Marie Weatherman's books on glass—

COLORED GLASSWARE OF THE DEPRESSION ERA *($10)*

COLORED GLASSWARE OF THE DEPRESSION ERA 2 *($25)*

PRICE TRENDS: Supplement to
COLORED GLASSWARE OF THE DEPRESSION ERA 1 & 2
   (published annually; write for this year's description and price)

FOSTORIA: ITS FIRST FIFTY YEARS *($15)*

FOSTORIA PRICE WATCH *($4)*

can be obtained from the author and publisher:

Weatherman GLASSBOOKS
P.O. Box 4444 Springfield, Missouri 65804

**Printed in the United States of America 1976
International Book Number 0-913074-00-4**

Table of Contents

This book is for my readers

Acknowledgements

Certainly I want to thank the glass companies whose help proved so invaluable to me in my research:

Anchor Hocking Glass Company (Hocking Glass Company), Lancaster, Ohio

Bartlett-Collins Glass Company, Sapulpa, Oklahoma

Continental Can Company (Hazel Atlas Glass Company), Clarksburg, West Virginia

Corning Glass Works (Macbeth-Evans Glass Company), Charleroi, Pennsylvania

Federal Glass Company, Columbus, Ohio

Imperial Glass Company, Bellaire, Ohio

Indiana Glass Company, Dunkirk, Indiana

Jeannette Glass Company, Jeannette, Pennsylvania

Westmoreland Glass Company, Grapeville, Pennsylvania

In addition, many of my good friends were of especial help to me while I was deep in the production of the Second Edition. They loaned me dishes to photograph, aided me in my extensive collecting and contributed valuable information. All of them—most important to me!—really **cared** about this book. Thank you Alice Wilson, Ruby Hall, Fern Angus, Janice Wheeler, Anna Mae Williams, Ann Hall, Charlene White, Blanche McKinney, Lorane Woolery, Ona Hanes, Donna Woods, Mildred Henson, Grace Williams, Ilene Lee, Helen Jeffrey, Lois Frisbie, Idell Buckby, Marguerite McGuire, Joyce Medford, Mary Jo Blust, Bobby Meyers, Mr. and Mrs. Fred Ray, Mr. and Mrs. Robert W. Brown, Mr. and Mrs. B. Oscar Brown, Mr. and Mrs. David M. Brown, Mrs. Anna Weatherman, Mr. W. L. Olson, and Mrs. John F. White.

There are three more people whom I want to thank, but the enormity of this task leaves me wordless at the last. Vernon, my husband, and my daughter Suzanne, who attends the University of Missouri, aided greatly in production and kept the home fires burning, and my daughter Annette, who is an English major and graduate student at Harvard University—well, without Annette, "ain't no way I could 'a wrote this here book."

Foreword to the First Edition,
Colored Glassware of the 1920's and 1930's

"Colored glassware" as it is used in this book refers to that distinctive kind of transparent glass made in colors — primarily in pink, green, and amber — and molded into a great variety of different patterns during the late 1920's and early 1930's. Care should be taken not to confuse it with older antique glassware, especially since pattern names are sometimes identical. It is nearly impossible to describe this glassware in such a way as to distinguish it unquestionably from other, similar types; one almost has to see it to recognize its characteristic qualities. The best way to identify it, of course, is by color, which is nearly always uniform, and by pattern.

You may have heard this glassware referred to as "Depression Glass"; it was, of course, made and sold primarily during those lean years. Through subsequent years of what was probably constant use, the delicate pieces were broken or lost until most households soon owned only a few odd pieces instead of the original full set. Then, some years ago, there was a trend to construct mosaics from purposely shattered colored glass, diminishing the number of pieces still further. But at some time between the demise of that practice and the present, certain people began to realize that the old glassware had a special beauty and history. Colored glassware of the 20's and 30's had been discovered; the next few years saw scores of men and women everywhere become collectors of it. Their motives were the preservation as well as the enjoyment of the glass; reassembled sets are now being passed on to children as treasured possessions, preserving its history and graceful beauty for the enjoyment of coming generations.

Today, antique stores are beginning to sell the colored glass. But more important, pieces of it are even now going unnoticed in cupboards, attics, and secondhand stores, its true value unknown. This value has already increased significantly in the last few years; tomorrow, the glassware shall certainly join the ranks of other antique glass, such as pressed or Carnival. That is, of course, why this guidebook is needed today, rather than tomorrow — now, while the glass is still available to all who would be collectors.

Although most enthusiasts certainly consider their completed sets to be "collector's items," they often actually use them. Some set their Sunday dinner table with them. Others use them in decorating, to carry out a color scheme, for example. But I really think that most people, starting out with a few pieces inherited from Grandmother, eventually discover, as I did, the intrinsic beauty of the glass in its variety of patterns, and become preservers of the glassware for its own sake.

It is that enthusiasm which has inspired me to publish this guidebook. As far as I know, it is the first to be written on this facet of antique glass collecting. It will not be the last, nor will it be the best; for here I have sacrificed a more thorough research to the demands of the time and the public. Collectors of this glassware now exist in such numbers that some kind of guidebook — be it but a preliminary one — which functions to establish certain conventions (such as pattern names, for example) becomes necessary to prevent the confusion which so often results. Different sections of the country, to quote the best example, sometimes have different names for the same pattern — and many patterns have no known name at all — making communication between collectors (or between collector and dealer) virtually impossible. Let this, then, be that first guidebook; let it serve as common ground for confirmed enthusiasts and as an introductory guide for new and prospective ones.

I am well aware — and so should be the reader — that much of this book is the recording of convention rather than of historical fact, and that there are surely some missing pieces and missing patterns. But the obstacles that must be overcome to unearth the "historical fact" (such as when and where a particular pattern was made, which pieces were made in it and in what colors, and its rightful name) are almost insurmountable. That there is a dearth of historical material on the subject is not surprising. When colored glassware made its advent in the late Twenties, it was not considered important. It sold as inexpensive, everyday dinnerware, in dime stores and by such companies as Sears, Roebuck and Montgomery Ward, or, like Carnival glass, was given away as premiums at fairs or in boxes of tea and oats. Perhaps the fanciful patterns never became popular with the buyers, or perhaps the costs of production were too high to insure profit; at any rate, the "mold etched" process, as it was called, was a short-lived one lasting only into the early Thirties.

It is no wonder, then, that the manufacturing of this glassware was rarely ever recorded in any journal or catalog; no one foresaw its imminent popularity as a collector's item. That there is a distinct lack of documented evidence is understandable; I did examine what records I had access to, and I wrote to scores of glass companies in an effort to identify officially as many patterns as possible. I did not reach all the companies I had wanted (many of them are now defunct), nor did I travel the thousands of miles that would have been necessary to conduct an exhaustive research. This was largely because of the time factor, as I have stated before; I believe — and, I think, rightly so — that a thorough historical knowledge is second in importance to the current public demand for standardized nomenclature and means of identification. The historical fact I did glean from my limited research, then, is incorporated into the "data" conventionalized by the collectors themselves, to produce this guidebook in the hope that it will be of help to collectors new and old, and in all parts of the country, until a more thorough one can be undertaken.

H.M.W.

5 February 1969

Foreword to the Second Edition.
Colored Glassware of the Depression Era

One Year Later

I said I'd never write another book until all the research was complete, but just between you and me, one lives and learns. No research is ever complete. There is always more to dig out, if one just keeps digging, and it so happens that public demand won't always wait until you're good and ready to publish.

Certainly I'd like to promise you a perfect book, but I cannot; our hobby is, and in all probability will be for some time, in a period of rapid transition. Only a moving picture could capture such a moving subject. The best I can do for you, then, is bring into focus the Depression Glass picture as it exists now.

In one year I've traveled those thousands of miles I once talked about—twice—in researching this edition, and I still haven't found out everything. But to my mind, there's no use worrying about what we don't have, when what we do have is the important thing. And we do have plenty to write about, after all. As our collecting hobby has grown, so has our knowledge of it. Today there is a wealth of new data—data which you should know.

So here it is, the new guidebook you asked for . . . because you need it. **Colored Glassware of the 1920's and 1930's** was, I think, a good beginning; **Colored Glassware of the Depression Era** will be, I hope, its worthy sequel.

One year later. When a new episode has begun to be written into the long history of glass collecting, much can happen in one short year. Yes, there's plenty to write about now: information we just didn't have a year ago. Out of the more than two hundred and fifty patterns illustrated, three-fourths now have official names or places of manufacture. The listings of pieces have been greatly refined.

In fact, those of you who re-read the "Foreword to the First Edition" just now no doubt will be struck by its naivete. To begin with, our colored glassware is not a 1920's phenomenon. A few patterns were designed as early as 1928 and 1929, and some small number even trickled into the early Forties, but the large majority of patterns were made during the years of the Thirties. These were, of course, the years made memorable by the Great Depression, and it is for this era that I have more appropriately titled the present edition.

Also, the patterns collectors are referring to as Depression Glass today were not exclusively made by the "mold-etched process," although it can be said that the "mold-etched process" was unique to the Depression era, and is therefore characteristic of it. But in addition to the large number of mold-etched patterns are those made by the "chip-mold," "paste-mold," "machine-pressed," and even "hand-made" methods of production. Some light is perhaps shed on these various processes in the "Introduction and Explanation of Terms."

Finally, that "dearth of historical material" I made so much of in the first "Foreword"—isn't. Now there aren't whole **books** on the subject, you understand, but a few days spent in a glass company's morgue do wonders for one's research if not for one's allergies. There are old catalogs and brochures, though not many, and not always; and there are even a few employees who remember old pattern names and assorted anecdotes, though these fine people won't be there forever.

I've been in those morgues and I've studied those catalogs and I've talked to the many people who each know a little bit—and I've put it all together, here, in this book. Oh, a few things are left out— some good stories, for instance, which don't exactly fit in here—but these I'll try to include in **Price Trends**, which will continue to carry yearly the current news about all our patterns as I receive it.

This brings me to a point which gives me a great deal of pleasure to make. Remember the paragraph from the original **Guidebook** that went like this?

> It should be remembered that in this book I have only written about that which I have seen or have seen evidence of, and, despite my years of collecting, there are still pieces, patterns, and colors which I have not yet seen. You may, for instance, find, in your Uncle Mack's pool hall, a pink Cameo fishbowl on legs—an item which I fail to mention in these pages. Should that occur, do not think that you have lost your mind, but sit down calmly and write me, telling of your discovery so that I can include it in future revisions, which are always necessary when writing a book of this kind.

Well, it was largely because of this paragraph that this Second Edition is here and now. No, nobody found the fishbowl, but you did sit down, and you did write—many, many of you. You told me what you liked about the first book and what you wanted to see in the next. You took the time to describe pieces, colors, and patterns which needed to be included in the future. You helped me with prices in your area—whether it was Alaska, Hawaii, any other state in the Union, or Canada.

By doing this, you helped everyone, because you helped shape the contents of this book—which may go to the four corners of the world before this is all over. You never know. Anyway, as I have said, this book is You as much as it is me. Your concern and enthusiasm for the glassware is reflected in these pages, and for this you have yourselves to thank. I want to thank you, too.

I had a good time writing this book, and perhaps I should ask you to forgive me for my lighthearted moments in the pattern discussions. But a collecting hobby—even one taken so seriously as collecting Depression-era glassware—is supposed to be fun; it is for me, and I suspect it is for you also. Put this book to work for you, then, in your collecting, but enjoy it, too.

And remember, if you and I ever meet someday in the back room of an old junk store—that pink Cameo fishbowl on legs is **mine!**

H. M. W.

February 5, 1970

Introduction and
Explanation of Terms

This book is simple in structure. In this chapter you will be introduced to some of the terms used by collectors of the period glassware. The glass companies which originated the colored ware are discussed in the second chapter. In the body of the book, seventy-eight major Depression Glass patterns are considered in alphabetical order according to name.

Heading each expanded pattern discussion is an italicized blurb which summarizes the essential facts for easy reference. One, two or three photographs illustrate each discussion, depending on the number of pieces and colors available in that pattern and its popularity. Concluding the description is a listing of that pattern's pieces. Usually the listing of each pattern's respective pieces can be said to be "official" in that it was obtained from the original catalogs or records of the company which made it. However, such a list, while being "official," might not necessarily be complete — the catalog of that specific year might not have listed all the pieces actually made. This should be kept in mind.

In most cases the names of the patterns are official; that is, they were so called by their manufacturer. Often enough, however, nameless patterns have been christened some name or other by their collectors, and are therefore alphabetized by these conventional names. Such cases are indicated in the text. Also indicated at the start of the italicized blurb are old, conventional names where new, official names have since been found. A **pattern** or **line number** as used in this book refers to the numerical designation of a pattern by its maker.

19

Different companies called their pieces by various terms, and in each case I have tried to maintain the original term used. Pitchers are referred to as **jugs, ball jugs,** or **tilt jugs.** Round, shallow bowls are often called **nappies** (this term was "in" during the early Thirties); smaller ones are sometimes **cereal bowls.** Nappies with handles on two sides are **cream soups.** The 6" plate is listed as a **bread-and-butter** or a **sherbet** plate. A large serving plate may be called a **cake plate,** a **sandwich plate,** a **chop plate,** or a **salver.**

Reamers are orange, lemon, or grapefruit juicers. A **nite set** consists of a tumbler inverted on a handle-less jug. What might look like the bottom to a butterdish, but without any indentions for the lid, may be a **jam dish.** A **vegetable bowl** is an oblong bowl. **Grill plates** are what we often refer to as divided plates. Interestingly, compotes are listed by our companies as **comports** during the early Thirties.

The terms **dinner sets, luncheon sets, breakfast sets, and bridge sets** are supposed to designate the size of a set. They are used in this book as they were used in original catalogs of each particular pattern, but I don't try to define them for you here since it would seem that the terms were applied almost arbitrarily.

Our Depression Glass, especially that made by Hocking, Federal and Hazel Atlas, was often used as **promotional items** or **premiums.** **Oatmeal glass** refers to "Sandwich" or other patterned glass which was used as premiums in boxes of oatmeal. **Open stock** items are those which were sold individually as well as (or rather than) in sets.

Almost all of the Depression glassware we collect was made by machine. Of these, some were made by the **chipped-mold** method, some by the **paste-mold,** some by the **cut-mold,** and some by the **mold-etched** techniques. "Mold-etched" is the process by which a pattern is etched with acid into the iron mold itself, rather than directly into the glass. Since so many of our patterns are of this type, I have included below a detailed description of how the molds were made.

The pattern to be etched into the mold is first laid out on a steel plate which has been covered with an acid-resistant wax. The pattern is cut through this wax and the plate is then treated with an acid bath. This cuts the pattern into the steel. After being cleaned, the figure is then filled with the wax to the surface of the plate. The wax figure can then be lifted from the plate by means of tissue transfer paper. If the figure is a "repeat" motif it is only necessary to cut one unit into the plate and successive wax impressions are taken from this master plate. The tissue transfers are then laid out in their final positions in the mold cavity, and the tissue backing is removed by warming it. This leaves a negative wax impression laid out in the mold. Interstices between the pattern units are hand-painted with the wax resist.

The next step is the actual etching of the iron mold. This is accomplished by filling it with acid which eats away the surface not covered with resist. When the figure has been cut to the proper depth, the acid is poured off and the wax is removed with solvents. The mold is now ready for production.

Glass made from these molds can usually be identified by the fact that the pattern stands in relief on the glass surface and has the characteristic roughened surface of acid-eroded iron. Any workable glass can be formed in the molds.

A few patterns of Depression Glass were hand-molded rather than made by machine. Examples are Westmoreland's "English Hobnail" and Indiana's "Sandwich" design.

Pot glass and tank glass refer to the way glass was melted. **Pot glass** is that which is melted in open or covered pots in a furnace that may contain different colors. Pot glass is almost never used for machine productions. **Tank glass** is that which is melted in a tank which contains only one color, and usually melts continuously. That is, a new glass batch may be fed in at the back while workmen are working out of the front.

Rose, Rose Pink, Rose Marie, Rose Tint, Rose Glow, Nu-Rose, Wild Rose and **Flamingo** all describe, more or less, the pink glassware synonymous with the period. The characteristic green color is advertised as **Springtime Green** by Federal, **Emerald Green** by Hocking, **Imperial Green** by Imperial, and just "green" by others. Depression-era glassware comes in several versions of yellow, ranging from topaz (yellow) to amber. **Golden Glow** is Federal's term for an amber color. **Ritz Blue, Dark Blue,** and **Deep Blue** are all what is sometimes referred to as **Cobalt Blue. Madonna** is Federal's medium blue. **Ultra-marine** is Jeannette's dark blue-green color. **Delfite** is the soft blue, opaque ware also made by Jeannette. It is sometimes referred to as "blue milk glass," but strictly speaking the term is not appropriate. **Monax, Cremax** and **Ivrene** are Macbeth-Evans' opaque white, cream, and ivory colors, respectively.

Amethyst is a purple tint. **Burgundy** is a purple tint, nearly the same as amethyst, used by Hazel Atlas. **Satin Finish** is a treatment rather than a color; it can be applied to any transparent glass. The special acid-etching results in a cloudy or frosted translucence. **Black** is black opaque glass popular in the early Thirties. It was cast in a few of the Depression Glass molds. The **ruby red** color of "American Sweetheart" is different from the darker **Royal Ruby** glassware made by Hocking during the period and later. All companies referred to clear glass as **Crystal.**

The dates attributed to the patterns are derived from old catalogs, line numbers, and other records, and thus in many cases are approximate. Also, the fact that a pattern is described as having been discontinued in a certain year does not mean that it couldn't have been sold subsequently. That a piece, pattern, or color is **scarce** may be due to the fact that little was made, or that it is being widely collected. What is labeled "scarce" today and what will be "scarce" ten years from now may not be the same at all. A **reissue** is a piece or pattern which has been reproduced at some later date from the same mold used earlier.

After the extensive coverage of the major patterns, I have included in this book a section which treats occasional or "conversation pieces." In the section you will see these special-interest pieces of unidentified make or date, as well as of known manufacture, which do not correspond to any of the previously listed patterns. In addition, this chapter will include "occasionally found" pieces or examples of tableware lines made by known or unknown companies which are not being collected to any significant degree today (and hence are not included in the main body of this book).

Finally, an index is included which lists conventional pattern names as well as official ones providing you a ready cross-reference to facilitate your finding a pattern in these pages.

*   *   *   *   *

Perhaps you've noticed that I have not as yet defined **Depression-Era Glassware.** That is because I don't think I can. Is it defined strictly by date? by color? by pattern? by company? by method of manufacture? by the "kind" of glass? or by the fact that it is being collected today under the name "Depression Glass"? It could be the case that only this last is a safe-enough description. However, I will proffer a tentative "definition" of our subject. I would say that **Depression Glass** is the relatively inexpensive glassware which is recognized as that which was made in colors, primarily by machine, and sold during (or very near) the years of the Great Depression, and which is being collected as such today.

Discussion of Glass Companies
and their Characteristics

After my research trips East this past year, I was able to look back over what I had learned at the various glass factories and make some interesting generalizations about them and their involvement with the Depression glassware. In order to share this overview with you, I will take time now to relive the journeys as I made them, taking you along with me, as it were, in the hope that you too will gain a better perspective on the entire Depression-era glassware picture.

From St. Louis I headed east to the little Indiana town of Dunkirk to visit the **Indiana Glass Company.** I was the guest of Mr. A. L. Harshman, assistant to the plant manager, who explained that Indiana is the only glass company producing both hand and machine made glassware in the same factory.

In 1929 Indiana had been making pressed patterns and hand-molded "Sandwich" in crystal and was beginning to experiment with pink and green as colors for tableware. These early pink and green pressed lines (such as "Tea Room") were of heavy and serviceable glass. The patterns were nameless and originally sold by line number. By the close of the Twenties, Indiana was beginning to use a "mold-etched process" to etch delicate patterns onto glassware, and came out with "Lorain," "Vernon," and "Number 612" in crystal, green, and yellow. But it was then that the Depression hit, and the company was forced to discontinue its fanciful lines after a few short years. These were the only three mold-etched patterns to be issued by Indiana.

However, the company continued to produce "Sandwich" design, casting it also in pink and green glass in the early Thirties. Two more pressed patterns listed in this book, "Daisy" and "Pineapple and Floral," were successful enough in crystal that some of the molds from the original lines have been used for reissue through the years to the present. In the Indiana morgue are preserved samples of its Depression Glass patterns, including the red "Sandwich" nappies which had been made for the Chicago World's Fair in 1933.

Leaving the industrious Indiana factory isolated in the rolling Hoosier hills, I continued on to the **Federal Glass Company,** located at Columbus, Ohio. I was assisted in my research at the great sprawling plant by four men, now Federal officials, who had actually worked with the company at the time our glassware was being made. Mr. G. H. Kuse had named the "Diana" pattern after his daughter. Mr. Vernon Nicholson and his brother were etchers who worked on all the mold-etched pattern molds. Mr. W. N. Davis remembers spraying the amber carnival color on "Normandie," and Mr. Henry Kielmeyer tells a good story about the "Parrot" pattern (page 130). It was through the combined efforts of these men, who pooled their old brochures, samples, and remembrances, that enough evidence was found to document Federal's Depression Glass history.

Although Federal made a practice of naming all its patterns, some of these names have become lost. This is because Federal in the years of the pinch didn't publish catalogs or otherwise record its earlier productions.

In the late Twenties Federal began working green tanks of glass. In addition to restaurant supplies, tumblers, and kitchenware, the company was making a few lines of green tableware by machine. The patterns were "Pear Optic" and other "Optics," and "Colonial Fluted." These earlier issues carried the Federal mark (the letter F in a shield). The factory fashioned its first mold-etched design, "Georgian," in 1931, and this pattern also was made only in green. In subsequent years, four more mold-etched patterns were made—"Parrot," "Madrid," "Patrician," and "Normandie," in that order. The colors made and advertised then were "Springtime Green," "Rose Glow," "Golden Glow," "Madonna Blue," crystal, and iridescent amber.

Then in 1934 the "chipped-mold" method was used to make "Mayfair," "Rosemary," and "Sharon," in that order. "Diana," another pressed pattern, was produced, as were open-stock pitchers, tumblers, and occasional pieces. Toward the last years of the Thirties, Federal used still another method of manufacture, the "paste-mold method," to make "Columbia" and "Heritage" in crystal.

The next day I drove into the huge **Anchor Hocking** complex in Lancaster, Ohio. Guards directed me to "Plant #1" where our glassware had been made forty years ago. There I met Mrs. Vonda Stuckey, who was to assist me so greatly in my research.

The many patterns made by this company (which was simply "Hocking Glass Company" at that time) were sold by both name and line number. In the year 1929, Hocking was making its first tank-colored glassware as were other companies at that time. They made kitchenware, such as large salt-and-pepper sets, flour, sugar, tea, and coffee containers, reamers and measuring cups, refrigerator bowls, mixing bowls, and tumblers, all in green.

Hocking's first colored tableware was also made in this year—green "Circle" design. It was followed by "Spiral," "Block Optic," and "Ring." In 1930 the company's first mold-etched pattern, "Cameo," was designed and introduced, followed by "Princess" and "Mayfair." By this time yellow tanks of glass had been added and most of these patterns were issued in Topaz. In the years to follow, Hocking made its pressed patterns ("Old Cafe," "Lace Edge," "Miss America," "Queen Mary," "Colonial," "Hobnail," "Waterford," "Manhattan," "Coronation," "Roulette," "Oyster and Pearls," and "Sandwich," in that order) concurrently with its three mold-etched patterns until the late Thirties. The pink tanks of glass were added in 1932, and many of these patterns were cast in pink. Also, Hocking had a penchant for treating assorted pieces of its patterns with a special acid-etched process which resulted in an effect called "Satin Finish." These translucent pieces often were hand-painted with floral motifs. They were primarily promoted at holiday time.

Hocking did a rousing business in its colored glassware. For example, I read that one Chicago store had sold 10,000 nineteen-piece water sets in "Cameo," at $1 a set, in just three days of special sale. In one month, 25 carloads of these same water sets were sold.

In 1937, Hocking and a group of other glass companies consolidated to become the Anchor Hocking Corporation. Anchor Hocking continued the last few patterns listed above until the end of the decade.

Hocking's morgue was large and complete. In it I saw the cover to the "Mayfair" sugar bowl in pink, and a "Mayfair" vase in green. These two pieces are not listed in old catalogs, nor are they seen "in circulation" today.

I left Lancaster for Cambridge, Ohio, to find out all I could about the Cambridge Glass Company, now defunct. Cambridge did hand-mold pink and green glassware at the time other factories did. The ware was often decorated with gold, and many occasional pieces were made. Most pink and green Cambridge Glass carries the trademark (a small c inside a triangle). After 1935 the company made their glass without the symbol because they felt it was too ostentatious for tableware.

I had learned that the Cambridge records are now owned by the **Imperial Glass Company,** as are the old Heisey catalogs, so my next jaunt was to Bellaire, Ohio. As had Cambridge, the Heisey and Imperial companies had made large amounts of pink, green, and yellow glass from as early as 1926 up until 1936. Imperial introduced its pink color as "Rose Marie" and its green as "Imperial Green." One or two of the early Imperial patterns are included in this book. In general, the handmade glassware of these three companies is not treated fully here since other books are being written on these subjects. Examples of the ware, however, can be seen on page 184.

The situation was much the same at Pittsburgh, Pennsylvania, where the **United States Glass Company** had made a considerable amount of pink and green glassware in the late Twenties. (The factory was ruined by flood and fire in the middle Thirties.) None of the major patterns in this book, however, have been attributed to this company, although a few pieces verified to be of U.S. Glass make can be seen on page 198. It is believed that this company made most of the Shirley Temple pieces.

The tall smokestacks I spotted while driving into Jeannette, Pennsylvania, turned out to be part of the old Jeannette factory where Depression patterns were made. I continued on, however, to the old McKee site where the modern **Jeannette Glass Company** is located today. (In 1951, McKee became the Thatcher Glass Company. In 1961, the Jeannette Glass Company bought it and moved there.)

At the Jeannette plant I was kindly aided by Mr. P.G. Sailer, the president of the company, and by Mrs. M. Hermann, Mr. M. Gregory, and Mrs. S. Abraham. Together we sketched the long history of Jeannette's involvement with Depression-era glassware.

In 1929, the company had been making such crystal patterns as "Iris" and "Intaglio" in crystal, and plain pitchers and tumblers in pink. "Cubist," a pressed pattern, was the company's first complete line of pink tableware. Jeannette's first mold-etched patterns, beginning with "Floral" and "Cherry Blossom" in 1930, were successful from the start, and "Adam," "Doric," and "Doric and Pansy" followed in the years throughout the Thirties. Other pressed patterns after "Cubist," listed in order of their making, are "Sierra," "Windsor," "Swirl," and "Homespun." Later in the forties, a few more pressed patterns (such as "Holiday" and "Anniversary") were issued.

Pink, which Jeannette often called Wild Rose, and green were the company's first two colors. Delfite (opaque blue) and Jadite (opaque green) were developed in the mid-Thirties and made into tableware and kitchenware. A blue-green shade, Ultra-Marine, was processed in 1937, and an iridescent amber color was introduced still later. Jeannette's Depression Glass patterns were not made in yellow or amber.

Jeannette often repeated the styles of its handled bowls, sandwich trays, and candlesticks from pattern to pattern. It did not make cookie jars with its sets of tableware, and it was the only company to make cone-shaped pitchers and child's sets in the Depression Glass.

Jeannette made a large amount of kitchenware through the years, and novelties such as powder jars (the ones with the animal figures on the cover) and candy containers. Jeannette was such a big

29

distributor that it advertised some of its items as to be "sold by carload only."

While at Jeannette I examined the McKee catalogs, in which I found that they, too, had made pink and green tableware, fountain supplies, and reamers in the late Twenties. However, this tableware was primarily etched or gold-encrusted, and none of the major patterns in this book are attributed to McKee manufacture. During the Depression, McKee specialized in the characteristic opaque ware which is being collected today in French Ivory, Jade Green, and Poudre Blue. As I toured Jeannette's morgue I was surprised to see "Iris" in pink and green (two colors which are not being found in "Iris" today). I also found a sample of a beautiful pink pattern which I had never before seen, and it was explained that this pattern had never been released.

After spending a couple of days at Jeannette, I moved on to Grapeville, Pennsylvania, and **Westmoreland Glass Company**. Here Mr. J. H. Brainard, the president of the company, and Mr. D. V. Johnson helped me in my research. It was found that Westmoreland had contributed at least two of the patterns of this period glassware, "English Hobnail" and "Princess Feather" (Sandwich), which were both hand-molded in pink and green.

The next day I set out for Charleroi, Pennsylvania, to visit Corning Glass Works which had been the site of **Macbeth-Evans Glass Company** in the years of the Depression (the two had merged in the latter part of 1936). Mr. G. Vincent, Mr. A. M. Gossie, and Mrs. M. Beazell met me there with the appropriate Macbeth catalogs in hand.

Prior to 1929, Macbeth had been making crystal glassware primarily by hand. But machine methods were beginning to make the scene, and Macbeth started making colored tableware, mostly in pink. Macbeth never made as much green as the other companies did and used yellow in "S-Pattern" only.

"Dogwood," appearing in the late Twenties, was the company's first mold-etched pattern. It was followed by "Thistle," which was made from the "Dogwood" mold, "Petalware" (a pressed pattern), "American Sweetheart," and "S-Pattern," in that order The special Monax and Cremax colors were developed in order to

30

compete with the china and pottery industry in the early Thirties and were used in making "Petalware" and "American Sweetheart." The Ruby Red and Ritz Blue shades were introduced in the mid-Thirties in "American Sweetheart." In addition, Macbeth made "Roly Poly" tumblers, ice tubs, and cocktail shakers in these two colors.

The company made a practice of referring to its patterns by letter rather than by number or name. It made no candy jars, candlesticks, cookie jars, or butter dishes, and few pitchers. On the whole, the Macbeth glassware of the period was of a thinner, more delicate glass than that of other companies.

The last stop on my long trek was Clarksville, West Virginia, to research the **Hazel Atlas Glass Company.** (The Continental Can Company acquired Hazel Atlas in 1956; today, the company makes "Hazelware.") Mr. W. S. Franz, a Continental Can official, and Mr. W. N. Otto, an employee of Hazel Atlas at the time it was making colored glassware, contributed much helpful information.

During the first few years of the Depression era, Hazel Atlas made such pressed patterns as "Ribbon," "Moderntone," "New Century," and "Lydia Ray"; and such mold-etched patterns as "Cloverleaf," the two "Florentines," and "Royal Lace." Besides pink, green, and yellow, the company made Burgundy and cobalt blue. This company, as well as at least one other glass company, made Shirley Temple blue pieces, but how much is not known.

My journey over, I headed back to Missouri and home with the feeling that I had on the whole covered my subject rather well. All but a few of our patterns had been identified, and in most cases listings of colors and pieces had been obtained. Yes, the long trip had been worth it.

Major Depression Glass
Pattern Discussions

Adam

Jeannette Glass Co., 1932-1934; table settings in pink, green; mold-etched pattern

It seems quite natural that our story begin with **Adam,** as another, much older story once did. The pieces of this mold-etched pattern comprise one of the most complete lines of tableware made by Jeannette in the period between 1932 and 1934. Such extra items as the candy jar and cover, the candlesticks, the covered vegetable, and the vase, coasters, and ashtrays, made the set popular enough to sell many carloads of the pattern in the relatively short time it was in production.

Today the feathery design is most often found in pink, although it can also be collected in green. Some of the pieces have a round body with a flanged (square) rim to match the square plates. Square shapes, as will be seen, were popular in the period. Other pieces, such as the cone-shaped pitcher and glasses, relish dish, and candle-holders, are reminiscent of Jeannette's "Floral" pattern.

Adam was never reissued after the middle Thirties—not even in occasional pieces. Therefore, those polished, pearl-like pieces you are finding today are not new but are simply high-quality, well-preserved glassware. All in all, **Adam** is an apple in many a collector's eye.

ADAM LISTING

Plate, 9'' dinner
Plate, 9'' grill
Plate, 7¾'' salad
Plate, 6'' sherbet
Cup, round
Saucer, square
Bowl, 7¾'' nappy
Bowl, 9''
Bowl, 9'' covered vegetable
Bowl, 10'' oval vegetable
Bowl, 4¾'' nappy
Bowl, 5¾'' cereal
Platter, 12''
Sugar and cover
Creamer
Sherbet
Pitcher, 32 oz. jug, cone-shaped, 8'' tall
Tumbler, 7 oz., cone-shaped, 4½'' tall
Tumbler, 9 oz., cone-shaped, iced tea, 5½''
Relish Dish, 8'', 2-part oblong
Cake Plate, 10''
Butter Dish and Cover
Candy Jar and Cover, 2½'' low, round (cover same as sugar cover)
Candlestick, 4''
Salt and Pepper, 4'', footed
Ash Tray, 4½''
Coaster, 3¾''
Vase, 7½''

American Sweetheart

Macbeth-Evans Glass Co., 1930-1936; table settings in pink, translucent white; dessert sets in ruby red, deep blue, crystal; mold-etched pattern

Introducing their newest dinnerware design, Macbeth-Evans in a 1930 catalog says, "The vogue of pink and the popularity of glass tableware combine to make this new Macbeth line a decided favorite in the feminine eye . . . Rose Pink Glassware is a complete line of tableware." The company, as was their convention, referred to it by letter — R Pattern — but its collectors have christened it **American Sweetheart.**

After appearing in "Rose Pink," the pattern was made in what is called "Monax," a translucent white which shows blue when held to the light. (Interestingly, some "Monax" plates have the center motif while others do not.) Then, around 1934, dessert sets (cream-and-sugar, 8" luncheon plate, cup-and-saucer and 12" cake plate) were made in "Ruby Red" and "Ritz Blue." The tidbit server, 15½" sandwich plate, and the 18" console bowl were not made in pink, but were made in red, blue, and "Monax."

Sometime in 1935 the company issued "Monax" again, this time adding a gold rim. A year later, they produced the pattern in "Cremax," an ivory color, to compete with the pottery trade. And at some time, the pattern was made in crystal and amethyst into ice

cream dishes with metal holders. Be sure to note that the pitcher and tumblers were made in pink only.

Macbeth was the only company to make **American Sweetheart,** and after 1936 they never reissued it. With its dainty, thin glass the lacy pattern is most popular today. The three special colors, the red, white, and blue, have stirred much excitement among today's Depression Glass compatriots.

AMERICAN SWEETHEART LISTING

Plate, 10" dinner
Plate, 9" luncheon
*Plate, 8" salad or dessert
Plate, 6" bread and butter
Plate, 11" chop plate
*Plate, 12" salver
Plate, 15½"
*Cup
*Saucer
Bowl, 9"
Bowl, 10" oval vegetable
Bowl, 6" cereal
Bowl, 3½" berry
Bowl, 4½" cream soup
Bowl, 10" soup, rimmed
Platter, 13"
*Sugar (cover on Monax only)
*Creamer
Sherbet, 4"; 4¼" low footed
Sherbet, ice cream in metal holder
Pitcher, 60 oz., 7½" (pink only)
Tumbler, 5 oz., 3½" (pink only)
Tumbler, 9 oz., 4" (pink only)
Tumbler, 10 oz., 4½" (pink only)
Salt and Pepper
*Console Bowl, 18"
*Tid-Bit Set, 2-tier, 8" plate and 12" plate
*Tid-Bit Set, 3-tier, 8" plate and 12" plate and 15½" plate

*Ruby Red and Ritz Blue

𝕬nniversary

Jeannette Glass Co., 1947-1949; table settings in pink, crystal; pieces in amethyst, milk white; pressed pattern

Strictly speaking, it cannot be said that **Anniversary** is Depression-era glassware since the first time it was made was in 1947. The shade of pink, however, is near that of the older glass, and it is being collected in sets; hence its inclusion here. Somewhat later, the line was issued in crystal, and pieces were made in amethyst and milk-white glass.

Some of the 1947-49 molds are still being used today to make Jeannette's "Diamond Cut" line in crystal and amber (a kind of carnival color). You can see it in their 1969-1970 catalogs. Not all the older pieces are being made today, however.

The pieces listed below are the ones advertised in 1947 under the original **Anniversary** name in pink only.

Plate, 9" dinner
Plate, 6¼"
Plate, 12½" sandwich
Cup
Saucer
Bowl, 9" fruit
Bowl, 7⅜" soup or cereal
Bowl, 4⅞" nappy
Sugar and Cover
Creamer

Sherbet
Wine Glass, 2½ oz.
Relish Dish, 8"
Butter Dish and Cover
Candy Jar and Cover, one pound
Comport
Cake Plate, 12½"
Tray or Pickle Dish, 9"
Vase, 6½"
Pin-up Vase

Block Optic

"Block"; Hocking Glass Co., 1929-1933; table settings in green, yellow, pink; pieces in satin finish; machine-pressed and blown pattern

We used to call this early 1929 pattern simply "Block," but original flyers advertising Hocking's new "thin-blown" glassware labelled it **Block Optic**. This first issue had a straight-sided cup and cream-and-sugar. The pattern was continued into the early 1930's and to the initial bare table and luncheon sets were added many extras. Now the cream-and-sugar came footed, and the cups were round.

Green was the color made most, though some small lines of pink and "Topaz" were tried in 1931 and 1932. By this time, some pieces had been dropped from all lines. A frosty "Satin Finished" cream-and-sugar, made around 1933, can be seen in the illustration.

Other companies made "block" designs but there are always differences. Hazel Atlas's "Block" (page 214), for instance, is a heavier glass.

Plate, 9" dinner
Plate, 8" luncheon
Plate, 6" sherbet
Cup, 2 styles
Saucer
Bowl, 7" nappy; 8¾" nappy
Bowl, 5¼" nappy or cereal
Bowl, 4¼" nappy
Platter, 10½"
Sugar, three styles: cone-shaped; round, footed; straight sides
Creamer, three styles: cone-shaped; round, footed; straight sides
Sherbet, round; V-shaped
Sherbet, stemmed, 5" tall
Pitcher, 52 oz. jug, 8½"
Tumbler, 5 oz. juice, 3"
Tumbler, 9 oz.
Tumbler, 10 oz. iced tea
Tumbler, footed, 10 oz. iced tea; footed, 9 oz.
Goblet, wine, 4"
Goblet, 6"
Butter Dish and Cover, round; oblong, 3" x 5"
Candy Jar and Cover, 6½", tall; 2½", low
Candlestick, 1¾"
Salt and Pepper
Ice Tub
Reamer, orange
Nite set, 6" high; tumbler 3"

Bowknot

Of unknown manufacture and date; pieces in green, crystal; mold-etched pattern

This pattern has no known manufacturer or name so collectors call it **Bowknot** unofficially. The very few pieces which have turned up so far seem to indicate that the pattern will prove to be a luncheon set, without a cream-and-sugar. Those who are trying to amass one-of-each-pattern will be able to locate a plate, cup, or footed tumbler readily enough. **Bowknot** is mostly seen in green, but it was made in crystal, too.

Plate, 7" salad
Cup
Saucer
Bowl, 4½" nappy
Bowl, 5½" nappy
Sherbet, low, footed
Tumbler, 10 oz., 5"
Tumbler, footed, 10 oz., 5"

Bubble

Hocking Glass Co.; pieces in pink "Bullseye" in 1934; table settings in dark green and crystal in 1937; Anchor Hocking made light blue "Fire-King" in 1942-1948; pieces in milk-white "Provincial" in 1959-1960; table settings in ruby red "Provincial" in 1963-1965

Hocking has carried this pattern since 1934 in several colors and under different names. Perhaps it is best, then, to include it here under the name known to most collectors—**Bubble.** Please refer to the italicized heading for a record of which colors were made in which years under which names.

The only pink piece shown in catalogs is the 8⅜" fruit bowl advertised as "Bullseye" in 1934. The listing below is composed of this piece, the 1937 issue, and the 1942 "Fire-King" issue. In addition, I list the "Provincial" pitcher and tumblers which were added to the line in ruby red from 1963 to 1965.

Plate, 9¼" dinner
Plate, 6¾" bread and butter
Cup and Saucer
Bowl, 8⅜"
Bowl, 7¾" soup
Bowl, 5¼" cereal
Bowl, 4"; 4½" fruit

Sugar
Creamer
Platter, 12"
*Pitcher, 64 oz. ice lip
*Tumbler, 6 oz. juice
*Tumbler, 9 oz. old fashioned
*Tumbler, 12 oz.; 16 oz. iced tea

*Royal Ruby and late Crystal

Cameo

Hocking Glass Co., 1930-1934; table settings in green, topaz, crystal with platinum rim; pieces in pink; mold-etched pattern

Romantic **Cameo** was Hocking's first mold-etched ware, designed and named in 1930. The style of some of its pieces was fashioned from the successful "Block Optic" pieces made just previous to the introduction of this new laced-on line. This accounts for the resemblance between the candy jars, creams-and-sugars, wine glasses and goblets, and ice tubs in the two patterns. However, such new pieces were added to the green **Cameo** line as the cookie jar and cover, water bottle, relish dish, vase, 3-legged console bowl, and candlesticks. These items had not appeared in previous Hocking lines.

Cameo, then, was one of the largest sets on the market. Hundreds of carloads were sold. Two years later, the style of the cream-and-sugar and handles on the cup were changed. Notice that a cable design appears on the rim of some pitchers, while other rims are plain. In 1932, the pattern was made in "Topaz," but not in all pieces (see listing).

At some time, the company tried occasional **Cameo** pieces in crystal, and in crystal with a platinum rim, and in "Flamingo" pink. (The console bowl is one piece which has been found in pink to date.) Enthusiasts of this favorite pattern may find an original **Cameo** label on one of the pieces, as it is often preserved intact. Meanwhile, the little dancing girl continues to charm us all.

CAMEO LISTING

*Plate, 9½'' dinner
*Plate, 10½'' grill; 10½'' grill, closed handles
*Plate, 8'' luncheon
 Plate, 8'' square salad
*Plate, 6'' sherbet
 Plate, 10'' sandwich
*Plate, 10½'', closed handles
*Cup
*Saucer, same as sherbet plate
 Bowl, 5½'' nappy; 7'' nappy; 8¼'' nappy
 Bowl, 4¾'' cream soup
 Bowl, 9'' flanged soup
*Bowl, 9'' oval vegetable
*Bowl, 11'' console, 3-legged, flanged rim
*Platter, 10½''
*Sugar, 3''
 Sugar, 4''
*Creamer, 3''
 Creamer, 4''
 Sherbet, 3''
 Sherbet, thin, high stemmed, 5''
 Pitcher, 36 oz. jug, 5'' juice
 Pitcher, 56 oz. jug, 8½''
 Tumbler, 5 oz. juice, footed
*Tumbler, 9 oz., 5'', footed
 Tumbler, 11 oz., 6'', footed
 Tumbler, 5 oz., 3'' juice; 9 oz., 4''; 10 oz., 4¾''; 11 oz., 5''
 Goblet, wine, stemmed, 4''
 Goblet, stemmed, 6''
 Relish Dish, 7½'', three-part
 Cake Plate, 10''
 Butter Dish and Cover
 Cookie Jar and Cover,
 Candy Jar and Cover, 6½'' tall
*Candy Dish and Cover, 4'', low, fat
 Candlestick, 4''
 Salt and Pepper, 4''
 Water Bottle, 8½''; frosted (page 226), dark green (page 232)
 Vase, 8½''
 Ice Bowl, heavy, 3½''
 Jar and Cover, 2'' tall, closed handles
 Comport, 4'', footed, cone-shaped

*Known pieces in Topaz (yellow)

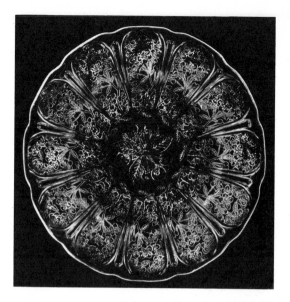

Cherry Blossom

Jeannette Glass Co., 1930-1938; table settings in pink, green, opaque blue; pieces in crystal; mold-etched pattern

When Jeannette tried their first mold-etched line of glassware in 1930, the result was a design so captivating that it was a favorite then as it is now—peerless **Cherry Blossom.** Perhaps the famous "Cherry Blossom Festival" inspired the name and design, since an early advertisement showed cherry trees blossoming by the Washington Monument in the capital city.

For eight years it was in their production—the mold is exclusively Jeannette's—and during that time the colors and shapes of some pieces varied. In the earliest sets, all the footed pieces had round bases, and the pitcher was cone-shaped, round-based, and with a border design only. Later, the bases were scalloped and the pitcher was made rounded (with either a round or a scalloped base) and with an all-over pattern. Tumblers had a border design; footed tumblers, with either round or scalloped bases, had an all-over design. Still a third style pitcher was made—straight and with a border design.

Molds for **Cherry Blossom** cookie jars, candy dishes, salt-and-peppers, relish dishes, or candlesticks were never made. The mug cup pictured was listed as an "8-oz. mug" and was made only in pink and green.

In 1936, **Cherry Blossom** was made in "Delfite" (Jeannette's opaque blue), but few carloads were distributed as compared to the pink and green. Since this glass is opaque, the mold-etched pattern

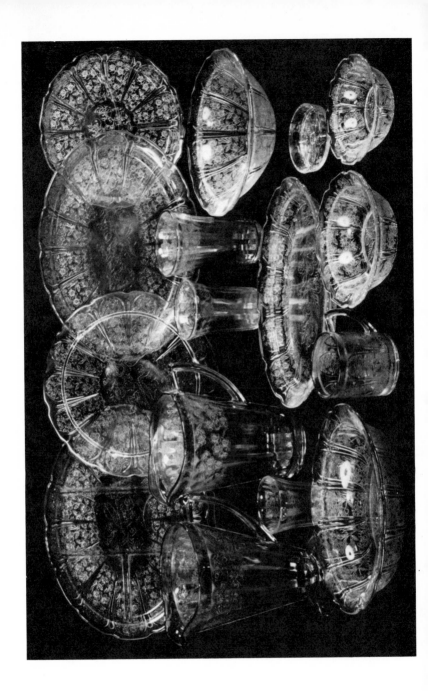

would not show through on such flat pieces as the plates and platters. Therefore an additional mold was required for the topsides of these pieces. "Delfite" was made in table settings, but the old catalogs do not show a butterdish, soup bowl, footed cake plate, or 3-legged fruit bowl as had been made in pink and green. And, if you are searching high and low for a "Delfite" sugar lid, you may as well relax—there isn't one listed.

If you have a **Cherry Blossom** sherbet plate which won't fit into the rest of your stack—you may have your first little plate to the child's set. Listed as "Jeannette's Junior Dinner Set," it was offered in pink and "Delfite." A set consists of 4 plates, 4 cups-and-saucers, and a cream-and-sugar, and is truly a little doll to own.

Somewhere along the line, a very few odd pieces were made in crystal. The green was discontinued about 1935, explaining the relative scarcity of this color. Jeannette's last catalog listing **Cherry** was in 1938, and it offered pink ware only. It is the only pattern to stay in production the entire Depression era.

CHERRY BLOSSOM LISTING

Plate, 9" dinner
Plate, 9" grill
Plate, 7" salad
Plate, 6" sherbet
Cup
Saucer
Bowl, 8½" nappy
Bowl, 9" handled
Bowl, 9" oval vegetable
Bowl, 4¾" nappy
Bowl, 5¾" nappy
Bowl, 7¾" soup
Bowl, 10½", 3-legged, fruit
Platter, 11"
Platter, 13"
Platter, 13", divided
Sugar and Cover
Creamer
Sherbet
Pitcher, 36 oz. jug, 6½", all over pattern
Pitcher, 36 oz., footed, cone-shaped, 8", pattern around top

Pitcher, 42 oz., straight sides, 8", pattern around top
Tumbler, 4 oz., 3½" juice, footed
Tumbler, 9 oz., 4½", footed
Tumbler, 5 oz., 3½", pattern around top
Tumbler, 9 oz., 4", pattern around top
Tumbler, 12 oz., 5", pattern around top
Cake Plate, 10¼"
Butter Dish and Cover
Tray, 10½" sandwich, handles
Coaster
Mug, 8 oz.

DELFITE LISTING

Plate, 9" dinner
Plate, 6" sherbet
Cup
Saucer
Bowl, 9", handled
Bowl, 9" oval vegetable
Bowl, 4¾" nappy
Platter, 11"
Sugar, no cover
Creamer
Sherbet
Pitcher, 36 oz. jug, 6½", all-over pattern
Tumbler, 4 oz., 3½", footed, all-over pattern
Tumbler, 9 oz., 4½", footed, all-over pattern
Tray, 10½" sandwich, handled

JEANNETTE JUNIOR DINNER SET

4 Cups
1 Creamer

4 Saucers
1 Sugar (no cover)

4—6" Plates

Cloverleaf

Hazel Atlas Glass Company, 1931-1935; table settings in green, pink, yellow, black, crystal; mold-etched pattern

Cloverleaf is listed under that name in old Hazel Atlas catalogs. First made in green and "Topaz" (yellow), it was later made in pink and then crystal. Also, luncheon sets were cast in the black glass popular during those years. Most of the salt-and-peppers in all colors are marked with the Hazel Atlas symbol.

Cloverleaf, a mold-etched design, was made in tableware but the line was not large. To avoid looking over any Depression-era "Clover" —take along your rabbit's foot.

Plate, 9" dinner
Plate, 10" grill
*Plate, 8" salad
Plate, 6" sherbet
*Cup
*Saucer
Bowl, 9" oval vegetable
Bowl, 5" nappy; 6¾" nappy
Bowl, 7" nappy
*Sugar

*Creamer
*Sherbet
Tumbler, 9 oz., 4"
Tumbler, footed, 10 oz., 5¾"
Candy Dish and Cover
*Salt and Pepper

*Known black glass pieces

Colonial

"Knife and Fork"; Hocking Glass Co., 1934-1938; table settings in green, pink, crystal; pressed pattern

It does look like the old "Knife and Fork" design, but Hocking named this pattern **Colonial** when they designed it in 1934. It was molded in pink, green, and crystal glass. The heavy line with its larger-than-usual pieces does remind one of the glassware that set the table of early Americans in the days of the Colonies.

The listing below is official, using the original names of the items. Notice the variety of tumblers and goblets. The 18-oz. pitcher which one would think is the creamer is actually listed as a "milk pitcher." The celery or spoon holder (as it is listed) is quite unique in this period glassware.

In **Colonial**, Hocking has experimented with a different shade of green. It contains more yellow than did, say, green "Princess" or "Cameo," which preceded it. The stately line was discontinued in 1938 and never reissued; unfortunately, it is not plentiful today.

Plate, 10" dinner
Plate, 10" grill
Plate, 8½" luncheon
Plate, 6½" sherbet
Cup
Saucer
Bowl, 9" nappy
Bowl, 7" nappy or soup; 4½" cream soup
Bowl, 4½" nappy; 5½" nappy
Bowl, 10" oval vegetable
Platter, 12" meat
Sugar and Cover, large, 5"
Creamer, 8 oz. milk pitcher, 5"
Sherbet
Pitcher, 54 oz., 7"; 67 oz., 7½"
Tumbler, 1½ oz. whiskey, 2½"
Tumbler, 5 oz. juice, 3"
Tumbler, 9 oz.; 10 oz; 12 oz.; 15 oz.
Tumbler, footed, 3 oz. cordial, 3¼"
Tumbler, footed, 5 oz. claret, 4"
Tumbler, footed, 10 oz. cordial, 5¼"
Goblet, stemmed, 1 oz. cordial, 3¾"
Goblet, stemmed, 3 oz. cocktail, 4"
Goblet, stemmed, 2½ oz. wine, 4½"
Goblet, stemmed, 4 oz. claret or Rhine wine, 5"
Goblet, stemmed, 8½ oz., 5¾"
Butter Dish and Cover
Salt and Pepper
Celery or Spoon Holder, 5½"

Colonial Fluted

"Rope"; Federal Glass Co., 1928; table settings in pink, green; pressed pattern

In 1928 Federal Glass began its era of colored glass tableware with this pressed pattern in green. Later, around 1932, the company may have been experimenting with the new pink and blue colors, since pieces of **Colonial Fluted** in these two colors are reported from time to time.

However, the pattern wasn't as successful as the more decorative patterns which were being introduced, and **Colonial Fluted** was discontinued before any accessory pieces could be made.

Officials at Federal called the mold by the above name, but collectors sometimes nickname it "Rope" for the characteristic rope or cable effect in the border. It can be gathered in attractive luncheon sets.

Plate, 8" luncheon
Plate, 6" sherbet
Cup
Saucer
Bowl, 7½" nappy
Bowl, 6" nappy
Bowl, 4" nappy

Sugar and Cover
Creamer
Sherbet

Columbia

Federal Glass Co., 1938-1940; tablesettings in pink, crystal; paste-mold pattern

"Hail **'Columbia!' "** read the first advertisement of this Federal pattern in 1938. By 1939, the pink glassware trend had begun to pass and **Columbia** was made only in crystal. It was considered a short line, comprised of basic tableware only. The method of production used here was "paste-mold and pressed" by machine.

Collectors have recognized that this pattern is of late Depression-era production, and collect it today. The list below is as it appeared under the official name **Columbia** in Federal's old catalogs.

Plate, 9½" luncheon
Plate, 6" bread and butter
Chop Plate, 11¾"
Cup
Saucer
Bowl, 8½" nappy
Bowl, 5" nappy
Bowl, 8" open soup
Bowl, 10½" ruffled fruit
Butter Dish and Cover

Coronation

"Saxon"; Hocking Glass Co., 1936; table settings in pink; pieces in crystal, ruby red; pressed pattern

The berry set is the most easily found item in this pattern, since it was manufactured for a "special sales" promotion. **Coronation** was made for only a short time, and in only a few pieces—not even a cream-and-sugar is listed. Hocking produced its finely-mitred pattern in "Rose" and crystal, and in 1940, after the special berry set promotion, in "Royal Ruby" (page 161).

It turns out that this mold was not named for the "Saxon" kings after all, but we weren't far off. The official name as is specified in early catalogs is **Coronation.** That's keeping it in the royal family!

Plate, 8½" luncheon
Plate, 6" sherbet
Cup
Saucer
Bowl, 6½" nappy
Bowl, 8" nappy
Bowl, 4¼" fruit
Sherbet, 5¾ oz., low footed
Tumbler, 10 oz., footed, 5"

Cubist

"Cube"; Jeannette Glass Co., 1929-1933; table settings in pink, green, crystal; pressed pattern

Cubist in pink and green was one of the first of our Depression Glass patterns to be made by Jeannette. The green line was soon discontinued, however, which explains the shortage of it today. Crystal was added to the production line a few years later.

The larger-sized cream-and-sugar with cover, and such extra pieces as the candy dish, butterdish, and salt-and-pepper, were a part of this first production. Later, in the mid-Thirties, the 2" cream-and-sugar was made in pink and crystal, the latter primarily in sets on a round tray. At some later time, pieces in amber, olive green and milk-white were made.

Some people confuse Fostoria's "American" pattern for our Depression-era **Cubist**. However, the "American" has been hand-made, in crystal only, for the last fifty years. Listed below are the pieces of Jeannette's production only. Should you have crystal pieces not on the list, they could well be of Fostoria make.

Plate, 8" salad or luncheon	Tray, 7½", handles
Plate, 6" sherbet	Tumbler, 9 oz., 4"
Cup and Saucer	Sherbet
Bowl, 4½" nappy; 6½" nappy	Butter Dish and Cover
Bowl, 4½", deep	Candy Jar and Cover, 7½" tall
Sugar and Cover; Creamer, 3"	Salt and Pepper
Sugar and Creamer, 2"	Coaster, 3¼"

Daisy

Indiana Glass Co.; table settings in crystal in 1933; table settings in amber in 1940; pressed pattern

This is another early pattern which causes question today. The original mold was produced in crystal in the early Thirties, but has been reissued from time to time to the present. It is known to have been made in table settings in amber in the 1940's, and today certain pieces in olive green and milk-white are still being made.

Indiana calls it "Heritage" now, but it carried no name when first issued in 1933. The design is conventionally being called **"Daisy"** today, for the characteristic motif. Since it comes in table settings of crystal and amber, Depression Glass collectors like to include it in their repertoire. Below is a 1933 listing.

Plate, 9⅜" dinner	Bowl, 4½" berry; 6" cereal
Plate, 10¼" grill	Bowl, 10" vegetable, oblong
Plate, 8⅜" luncheon	Bowl, 4½" cream soup
Plate, 7⅜" salad	Platter, 10¾"
Plate, 6" sherbet	Sugar
Plate, 11½" cake or sandwich	Creamer
Cup	Sherbet
Saucer	Tumbler, 9 oz.; 12 oz.
Bowl, 7⅜"; 9⅜" deep berry	Relish Dish, 8⅜", 3-part

Diamond Quilted

Of unknown manufacture, early Thirties; table settings in pink, green, crystal; pressed pattern

Patterns like this are sometimes described in catalogs as "Diamond Optics." Its collectors, however, have labeled this **Diamond Quilted.** It is a beautiful pattern of excellent quality, and while there are few individual pieces, a finished set is a striking one.

Notice the handle of the cup. Its shape and position suggest that it was stuck on as an afterthought — but it is very comfortable to hold. The manufacturer of this set is not yet confirmed, but chances are good that it is Imperial. You may have pieces not listed below.

Plate, 8" luncheon
Plate, 7" salad
Plate, 6" bread and butter
Cup
Saucer
Bowl, 5" nappy; 7" nappy
Bowl, 4¾" cream soup
Sugar
Creamer
Sherbet

Goblet, 6"
Candlestick

Diana *Federal Glass Co., 1937-1940; table settings in pink, amber, crystal; pressed pattern*

The particular swirl pattern designated **Diana** by Federal was made in complete table services from 1937 until 1940, in pink, amber, and crystal. It can be distinguished from other spiral patterns because its pieces have two spiral motifs, one in the bottom or center and another on its rim or sides.

Evidently the pattern had been made earlier because it carries an older pattern number. When it was reissued in 1937, it was named **Diana** by a Federal employee for his daughter of that name.

Few supplementary pieces were made in this set, which is, I think, regrettable. The salt-and-peppers (not shown) are the same size and shape as those of the "Sharon" pattern (page 168). The cream-and-sugar are of an oblong shape, and a low candy dish with cover can be found.

A charming demitasse cup-and-saucer was made by Federal in a like swirl pattern, which some collectors may mistake as part of a child's set (non-existent in this pattern). The unique little piece comes in crystal, pink, and a lavender tint.

To compare fair **Diana** with other swirled patterns, see pages 174, 179 and 184.

Plate, 9½" dinner

Plate, 6" bread and butter

Plate, 11¾" cake

Cup

Saucer

Bowl, 9" nappy

Bowl, 11"

Bowl, 5" nappy

Bowl, cream soup, 5½"

Platter, 12" meat

Sugar

Creamer

Candy Jar and Cover

Salt and Pepper, flat lids, 2½" tall

Console Bowl, 12", scalloped edge

Ash Tray Coaster, 3½"

Demi-Tasse Cup 2 oz.; saucer, 4½" (as listed by Federal)

Dogwood

Macbeth-Evans, 1928-1932; table settings in pink, green, crystal; pieces in opaque white; mold-etched pattern

This was the first mold-etched pattern for Macbeth-Evans, arriving on the scene in pink in 1928. As is characteristic of this company, the imprint was designated by letter only. This was catalogued as "B Pattern," but Macbeth-Evans employees (now at Corning) say they never called it anything but **Dogwood.** Two of them vividly remember making **Dogwood.** Their job was to fashion the cream pitcher spouts by hand, which they did day after day. This accounts for the slight irregularities you have noticed in the lip of the thin creamer.

The fragile ware proved successful, so molds were prepared for machine production. A thicker cup and cream-and-sugar were made this time, and two styles of grill plates were added to the line. One had an all-over pattern, and the other had blossoms just on the rim. The extra-large cake plate was made in a thick, heavy glass. The pitcher and tumblers, which were plain in the original issue, were now adorned to match the rest of the line. Skilled Japanese were hired to apply the blossomy design by hand, using a silk-screen method. However, comparatively few pitcher sets were made in this style.

Notice that a two-tiered "tidbit set" with a metal handle, which is listed in pink, is not shown here. Keep in mind also that small variations exist in plate and bowl molds. The pink platter is a rare

piece in this pattern. Curiously, the ashtray shown on page 192 (lower right) was originally advertised with this pattern although it carried a different imprint.

The pattern was also cast in green, crystal, and opaque white, though in what amounts is not known. Certainly these colors are in scant supply today, which is unfortunate. **Dogwood** has a particular appeal for many collectors.

DOGWOOD LISTING

Plate, 9¼" dinner
Plate, 10½" grill, thick, 2 styles: pattern on rim, pattern all over
Plate, 8" luncheon
Plate, 6" bread and butter
Plate, 12" salver
Cup, 2 styles: thin and thick
Saucer
Bowl, 8½" nappy
Bowl, 9½" fruit
Bowl, 5½" dessert or cereal
Platter, 12"
Sugar, 2½" thin; 3" thick, footed
Creamer, 2¾" thin; 3" thick, footed
Sherbet, thin, low footed
Pitcher, 8", hand decorated
Tumbler, 10 oz., 4", plain
Tumbler, 10 oz., 4", hand decorated
Tumbler, 13 oz., 5", plain
Tumbler, 13 oz., 5", hand decorated
Cake Plate, 13", extra large, thick
Tid-Bit Set, 2-tiered, 8" plate and 12" plate, metal handle up center

Doric

Jeannette Glass Co., 1935-1938; table settings in pink, green; pieces in crystal, opaque blue; pressed pattern

This is another challenging pattern to assemble into sets, but its interesting pieces make this a worthwhile endeavor. Such pieces include the 8" oblong relish dish, and the 8" square tray which holds two 4" square and one 4" x 8" relish dishes as illustrated. This early issue (1935-1937) was made in pink and green.

In 1937, a small amount of **Doric** was made in "Delfite," the soft, opaque blue. Jeannette's last catalog listing the **Doric** line was in 1938, and the pattern was offered in crystal only. Much later, Jeannette made a few pieces in white glass from the old molds.

The 1938 catalog lists the comely **Doric** pattern under that name and in the following items.

Plate, 9" dinner	Creamer
Plate, 9" grill	Sherbet
Plate, 6" sherbet	Pitcher, 36 oz., 6"
Cup	Tumbler, 9 oz., 4½"
Saucer	Relish Dish, 8" x 8"; 4" x 8"; 4" x 4"
Bowl, 9" handled	Cake Plate, 10"
Bowl, 9" oval vegetable	Butter Dish and Cover
Bowl, 4½" nappy; 5½" cereal	Candy Jar and Cover, 8" tall
Bowl, 8¼" nappy	Salt and pepper
Platter, 12"	Sandwich Tray, 10", handled
Sugar and Cover	Ash Tray, 3½"; Coaster, 3"

Doric and Pansy

Jeannette Glass Co., 1937-1938; table settings in dark blue-green; pieces in pink, crystal; mold-etched pattern

This glassware was made in a singular "Ultra-marine" color in 1937, cast from the gracious **Doric and Pansy** mold designed by Jeannette. Pink and crystal was made too, but in such small amounts that one can hardly find it today. The blue-green pieces are not exactly in abundance, either, and if a cream-and-sugar in this pattern was ever made, I have never seen it.

The child's dinner set, advertised as "Pretty Polly Party Dishes," is in much demand today in pink and Ultra-marine. A set contains 4 cups, 4 saucers, one creamer, one sugar, and 4 six-inch dinner plates. It too was made in 1937 for about a year only. **Doric and Pansy,** by the way, is not an official name on this pattern, nor is the listing below the original one. (The child's set listing, however, is official.)

Plate, 9" dinner	Bowl, 4½" nappy
Plate, 6" sherbet	Bowl, 8½" nappy
Cup	Tumbler, 9 oz., 4½", pattern around top
Saucer	Sandwich Tray, 10", handled

Jeannette Junior Dinner Set
Pretty Polly Party Dishes

4 Cups	1 Sugar
4 Saucers	1 Creamer
4 — 6" Plates	

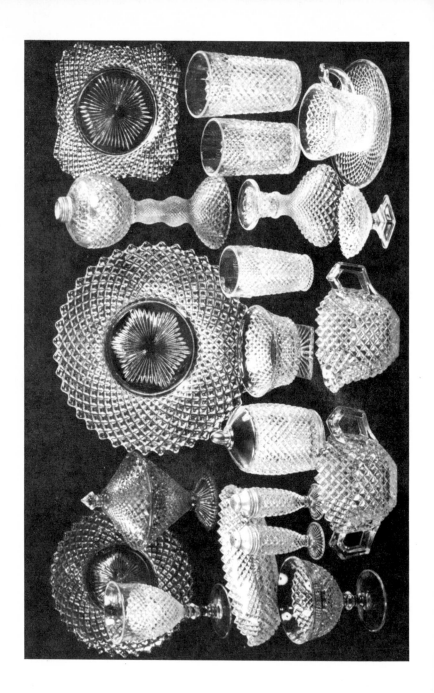

English Hobnail

Westmoreland Glass Co.; table settings in pink, green, and pieces in turquoise blue in 1928-1931; table settings in crystal for over fifty years; pieces in amber in 1925 and 1950

This hand-finished pattern has been made in crystal by Westmoreland for the last fifty years. The mold was already in use when the pink and green glass trend began in the late Twenties, so **English Hobnail** was then cast in those two colors and a turquoise blue. The pink and green came in complete luncheon and dinner services with many extra pieces, but are hard to find today.

Amber **English Hobnail** was produced in 1925 and 1926, and was reissued in the 1950's in a few items.

The pattern in crystal has been made more or less continuously from the earliest dates to the present. Sometime in the 1930's it was listed as having a black base. Today you can see the plain crystal advertised in Westmoreland catalogs, along with milk glass in a few pieces. The mold, however, is the original one.

Hocking's "Miss America" (page 119) is often confused with this pattern in both design and name. The differences can readily be seen in the center motifs and the blunted rather than pointed edges. The 1928-1931 issue of **English Hobnail** has round and square plates, round and square bases, and barrel-shaped stemware. Known pieces of this early issue made in colors are listed below.

Plate, 8"

Plate, 8" square

Plate, 10"

Plate, 6" sherbet

Cup and Saucer

Bowl, 8", 2-handled, footed

Tumbler, 5 oz., 3¾"; 10 oz., 4"; 12 oz., 5"

Goblet, 6¼"

Sugar

Creamer

Sherbet

Candy Dish and Cover

Relish Dish

Salt Dip, footed, 2" high

Salt and Pepper

Candlestick

Lamp

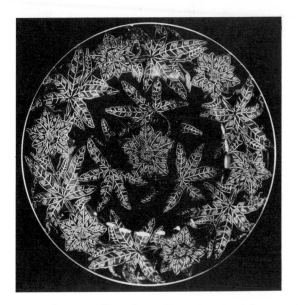

Floral

Jeannette Glass Co.; table settings in pink, green, in 1931-1934; pieces in opaque green in 1935-1936; mold-etched pattern

This Passiflora ("passion flower") pattern has been identified by Jeannette as their **Floral,** one of the earlier patterns made in our glassware. Today it is being collected in full table services plus such accessory pieces as the candy jar and cover, the covered vegetable, the family-sized salt-and-pepper, and the decorative candlesticks.

Characteristic of Jeannette's styling, the pitcher and tumblers are cone-shaped, and the sugar cover is interchangeable with the candy jar cover. **Floral** also boasts an extra-large lemonade pitcher. Notice too the 6" utility tray pictured, which is, I think, unique. All pieces were made in both pink and green.

Although the line was discontinued around 1934, a few pieces of what Jeannette called "Jadite"—an opaque green—was made in kitchenware a year later, which carried the leafy motif. If you can't find it on yours, look on the underside of the cover to your cereal set (it has coffee, sugar, tea, and cereal containers), and on the underside of the cover and on the bottom of the refrigerator dishes (page 230).

FLORAL LISTING

Plate, 9" dinner
Plate, 8" salad
Plate, 6" sherbet
Cup
Saucer
Bowl, 7½" nappy
Bowl, 8" covered vegetable, round
Bowl, 9" oval vegetable
Bowl, 4" berry
Platter, 10¾"
Sugar and Cover
Creamer
Sherbet
Pitcher, 32 oz. jug, 8", cone-shaped
Pitcher, 48 oz. lemonade, 10¼", cone-shaped
Tumbler, 5 oz. juice, footed, 4", cone-shaped
Tumbler, 7 oz., footed, 4¾", cone-shaped
Tumbler, 9 oz., footed, 5¼", cone-shaped
Relish Dish, 2-part, 5" x 6½" with handles
Butter Dish and Cover
Candy Jar and Cover (cover same as sugar cover)
Candlestick, 4"
Salt and Pepper, 4", footed
Salt and Pepper, 6", large
Ash Tray, 4"
Coaster, 3¼"
Tray, 6", closed handles
Vase, 5", 3-legged
Refrigerator Dishes, (page 230)
Cereal set, (page 230)

Old Florentine

"Poppy #1"; Hazel Atlas Glass Co., 1932-1934; table settings in green, yellow, pink, crystal; pieces in dark blue; mold-etched pattern

This fanciful etching graces a Hazel Atlas mold used to make table settings in "Killarney Green," "Topaz" (yellow), and "Sunset" pink. Crystal and a dark blue ware were tried, too, but little was made, especially in the latter.

This **Florentine** can be distinguished from the following "Florentine" variation in that its pieces have hexagonal shapes and serrated edges and bases. The **Florentine** name has been confirmed; however, the listing below may not be complete.

Plate, 9¾" dinner	Sugar, ruffled
Plate, 8" luncheon	Creamer
Plate, 6"	Creamer, ruffled
Cup	Sherbet
Saucer	Pitcher, footed, 36 oz., 6½"
Bowl, 9"	Tumbler, footed, 5 oz., 3"
Bowl, 9½" oval vegetable	Tumbler, footed, 9 oz., 4"
Bowl, 4" nappy; 6" nappy	Tumbler, footed, 12 oz., 5"
Platter, 11½"	Butter Dish and Cover
Sugar and Cover	Salt and Pepper

Florentine

"Poppy #2"; Hazel Atlas Glass Co., 1934-1936; table settings in pink, green, yellow, crystal; mold-etched pattern

The etching motif is the same—only the shapes of these pieces significantly differ from "(Old) Florentine" listed previously. Its pieces are round, and the plates have smooth edges as do the bases of the footed pieces. It was made in "Killarney Green," "Topaz," "Sunset" pink and crystal.

Sets are being augmented with extra pieces which keep turning up all the time. Notice in the picture the round tray with cream-and-sugar and salt-and-pepper, the oval meat platter with gravy boat, and the covered oval vegetable dish. The cone-shaped pitcher belongs to this set. The straight pitcher and tumblers pictured carry the **Florentine** motif and originally came as an extra water set.

A complete listing is not available for this pattern, but known pieces are recorded below. You may, of course, find other pieces in **Florentine.**

FLORENTINE LISTING

Plate, 9½" dinner
Plate 10½" grill
Plate, 8½" salad or luncheon
Plate, 6" sherbet
Cup
Saucer
Bowl, 8" nappy
Bowl, 5" nappy
Bowl, 9" oval vegetable and cover
Bowl, 4¾" cream soup
Bowl, 5" cream soup, ruffled
Platter, 11"
Platter, 11½", with gravy boat
Sugar and Cover
Creamer
Sherbet
Pitcher, 36 oz. jug, footed, cone-shaped
Pitcher, 54 oz. blown jug, straight sides
Pitcher, 80 oz. ice lip jug (not shown)
Tumbler, 5 oz., 3"
Tumbler, 9 oz., 4"
Tumbler, 12 oz., 5"
Tumbler, footed, 5 oz., 3¼"
Tumbler, footed, 9 oz., 4½"
Tumbler, footed, 12 oz., 5"
Relish Dish, 10", 3-partition, oblong
Butter Dish and Cover
Candy Dish and Cover, 6"
Salt and Pepper
Comport, 3½", ruffled
Candlestick, 3"
Coaster, 3"
Coaster Ash Tray, 5½"
Vase, 6"
Round Tray, 8½", Cream-and-Sugar and Salt-and-Pepper

Fortune

Hocking Glass Co., 1936-1937; table settings in pink, crystal; pressed pattern

Hocking made their **Fortune** in promotional glassware for cereal companies in the middle Thirties. It comes in pink and crystal. This is, of course, a conventional name only, and the listing below is unofficial.

Unfortunately, even the fortunate collector may find his **Fortune** hard to come by.

Plate, 8" luncheon
Plate, 6" sherbet
Cup
Saucer
Bowl, 4" nappy
Bowl, 4¼" nappy
Bowl, 4¼" nappy with handle
Bowl, 7¾" nappy
Tumbler, 9 oz., 4"
Candy Dish and Cover

Fruits

Of unknown manufacture, early Thirties; pieces in green, pink, crystal; mold-etched pattern

To date, no glass company has claimed **Fruits** as one of its old patterns. The design consists of pears, grapes, and cherries. The cherry motif in the bottom of the pieces is identical to the one appearing in the bottom of the "Cherry Blossom" tumblers made by Jeannette. Federal Glass Company made two patterns of tumblers which could be mistaken for **Fruits** except that one shows a pear as the only fruit and the other has a pear and grapes.

This pattern had to be old; a 1932 newspaper in Springfield, Missouri, advertised pieces in **Fruits** (for 2¢ each) as a special premium at the opening of a new five-and-dime store. Unfortunately, not many collectors will be able to gather **Fruits** today: it is simply scarce. It is most frequently found in green, but it was made in pink and crystal, too.

Plate, 8" luncheon
Cup
Saucer
Sherbet
Tumbler, 4", pear only
Tumbler, 4", pear and grapes

Georgian

"Love Birds"; Federal Glass Company, 1931-1935; table settings in green; mold-etched pattern

Federal's first mold-etched pattern is this, our old "Love Birds," which appeared under the name **Georgian** in an early catalog in 1931. This confirms the name which had been seen on original packing cases containing this pattern. **Georgian** was in production for several years; earlier, it was offered in full dinner sets and extras, and later, in luncheon sets with a smaller cream-and-sugar. This pattern, too, was a favorite promotional item.

The little love birds, which characterize it, are not easily detected at first, and don't appear at all on the 9-oz. tumbler or the 13-oz. iced tea, though the basket part of the motif does. Occasionally one finds a plate with only a rim design (one of these is included in the illustration). This glass is heavier than that of some other patterns, and has thick seams.

The original catalogs do not show a complete listing of pieces made, so whether the water pitcher, cake plate, or salt-and-pepper were ever made is open to conjecture. To my knowledge, they have never been seen. At any rate, be aware that the list below is unofficial. All pieces are in green only.

GEORGIAN LISTING

Plate, 9½" dinner
Plate, 9½" dinner, center and border design only
Plate, 8" luncheon
Plate, 6" sherbet
Cup
Saucer
Bowl, 6½", deep
Bowl, 7½" nappy
Bowl, 4½" nappy; 5¾" nappy
Bowl, 9" oval vegetable
Platter, 11"
Bowl, cream soup, handles
Sugar and Cover, 3" and 4"
Creamer 3" and 4"
Sherbet
Tumbler, 9 oz., thin 4", basket of flowers only
Tumbler, 12 oz. iced tea, basket of flowers only
Butter Dish and Cover
Hot Plate, 4", round, center design only

Heritage

Federal Glass Co., 1940; table settings in crystal; paste-mold pattern

Federal's **Heritage** is a later pattern, fashioned to resemble traditional old Sandwich Glass designs. It is of the "paste-mold and pressed" method of manufacture. **Heritage** came out just as the pink fad was on the wane, so was made in crystal table services only. Later, it was advertised in occasional pieces with a gold trim. It's being collected in attractive sets today.

Plate, 8" luncheon
Plate, 12"
Plate, 6"
Cup
Saucer
Bowl, 8½" nappy
Bowl, 10½" fruit
Bowl, 5" nappy

Hobnail

Hocking Glass Co., 1934-1936; table settings in crystal; pieces in pink; table settings in Moonstone in 1942; pressed pattern

Hocking produced this particular **Hobnail** in crystal in 1934, and this is the listing you will find below. Only four items—the 8½" plate, the footed sherbet, and the 6" saucer or sherbet plate and the cup— came in "Rose glass" (pink). These were made up especially for premiums in 1935, and discontinued in 1936.

Not until 1942 did Anchor Hocking introduce the "Moonstone" line, as production records show, which made use of the old **Hobnail** molds plus many new ones. An example of "Moonstone," an opalescent glass, can be seen on page 216. Finally, some of the molds were used to issue **Hobnail** in milk white as late as 1969.

*Plate, 8½" luncheon	Tumbler, 1½ oz.; 5 oz.; 9 oz.
*Plate, 6½" sherbet	Tumbler, 10 oz.; 15 oz.
*Cup	Tumbler, footed, 3 oz. wine
Saucer	Tumbler, footed, 5 oz.
*Sherbet	Goblet, 10 oz.
Bowl, 5½" nappy	Goblet, 18 oz. iced tea
Bowl, 7" nappy	Decanter, 32 oz. with ground stopper
Sugar	
Creamer	
Pitcher, 18 oz. milk	
Pitcher, 67 oz. jug	

*Pink

95

Holiday

Jeannette Glass Co., 1947-1949; table settings in pink; pressed pattern

One can see that Jeannette's happy **Holiday** was fashioned from the earlier "Windsor" molds (page 189), using the later style cream-and-sugar and footed tumblers. The 16-oz. pitcher is listed as a "milk pitcher," the 10½" plate as a "sandwich tray," and the 13⅝" plate as a "chop plate."

This pattern is a late one but is being collected today. Its pieces are of a slightly lighter pink than other patterns of the period, but a completed set is a becoming one indeed.

Jeannette's last catalog showing a complete **Holiday** line (1949) listed it in pink only. However, occasional pieces in milk white and iridescent amber (a sprayed-on color) were offered still later, and these you might find today.

Plate, 9" dinner
Plate, 6" sherbet
Plate, 13⅝"
Cup
Saucer
Bowl, 8½" fruit
Bowl, 5⅛" berry
Bowl 9½" x 7⅜" vegetable
Bowl, 7¾" soup or cereal
Platter, 11⅜" x 8"
Sugar and Cover

Creamer
Sherbet
Pitcher, 52 oz., 7" tall
Pitcher, 16 oz. milk, 4½" tall
Tumbler, 10 oz., 4"
Tumbler, footed, 4"; 6"
Butter Dish and Cover
Sandwich Tray, 10½"
Console Bowl, 10½"
Candlestick, 3"

Homespun

"Fine Ribbed"; Jeannette Glass Co., 1938-1940; table settings in pink; pressed pattern

Despite the fact that **Homespun,** previously called "Fine Ribbed," was made in complete table services, the delicate pattern is hard to accumulate today. Part of the reason is that the **Homespun** mold was used only two years before being converted into another pattern mold.

Notice that the platter to this set is meant to double as a tray. Originally, it is shown as a "jam set" with a cream-and-sugar and butterdish on it. Later, it is part of a "juice set" with six 4" footed tumblers. Note in picture the two styles of tumblers.

A beautiful pitcher to this pattern exists—somewhere. Unfortunately, one couldn't be found for the picture. It is round and squat and called a "tilt jug." You can see one much like it on page 224.

The child's "Tea Set" in **Homespun** consists of 14 pieces, and is a treasure-trove to Depression Glass collectors.

Plate, 9¼" dinner
Plate, 6" sherbet
Cup
Saucer
Bowl, 8¼" nappy
Bowl, 4¾" nappy
Bowl, 5" cereal or soup
Platter, 13"
Sugar
Creamer
Sherbet, low
Tumbler, 9 oz., 4"
Tumbler, 13 oz., 5¼"
Tumbler, 5 oz., footed juice, 4"
Tumbler, 9 oz., footed, 6"
Pitcher, 96 oz. ice tilt jug, fat
Butter Dish and Cover
Coaster Trays

HOMESPUN TEA SET

(Pink and Crystal)

4 Cups
4 Saucers

4 Plates, 4½"
1 Teapot and Cover

Honeycomb

Federal Glass Co., 1929-1932; table settings in green, pink; pressed pattern

As you can see, the pieces pictured under the common name **Honeycomb** all have similar patterns. At least the tumblers have been identified as being of Federal manufacture as they appeared in the old catalogs of that company. It is entirely possible that the cup-and-saucer and the cream-and-sugar were made by another factory. The pitcher carries a distinct motif on the bottom, so it, too, could have been made by someone else. **Honeycomb** resembles the hexagon "Optic" pattern of several companies.

You may well find additional pieces to the ones I have listed below.

Plate, 8" luncheon

Plate, 6"

Cup

Saucer

Bowl

Sugar

Creamer

Tumbler, 9 oz., 4"

Pitcher, 32 oz., 5"

Iris

Jeannette Glass Co., 1928-1932; table settings in crystal; pieces in pink, green; table settings in iridescent amber and crystal, 1950 and 1969; pressed pattern

Iris was made during the late 1920's, as recorded by Jeannette Glass Company, in crystal. Pieces in pink and green were seen in Jeannette's "morgue," but no records of such an issue for distribution are to be found.

The amber spray-on, carnival look-alike color was applied in 1950 and again in 1969. It is verified also that a full line of crystal **Iris** was reissued in 1969. Finally, pieces in white glass were being made in 1970.

Plate, 9" dinner
Plate, 8" luncheon
Plate, 5½" sherbet
Plate, 11¾" sandwich
Cup
Saucer
Bowl, 5" nappy
Bowl, 9"; 11" fluted
Sugar and Cover
Creamer

Platter
Sherbet, 3½"; 4"
Pitcher, 9½"
Tumbler, 4"
Tumbler, footed, 4" wine
Tumbler, footed, 5"; 6"; 7"
Butter Dish and Cover
Candlesticks, 2-branch, 5"
Vase, 9", crimped

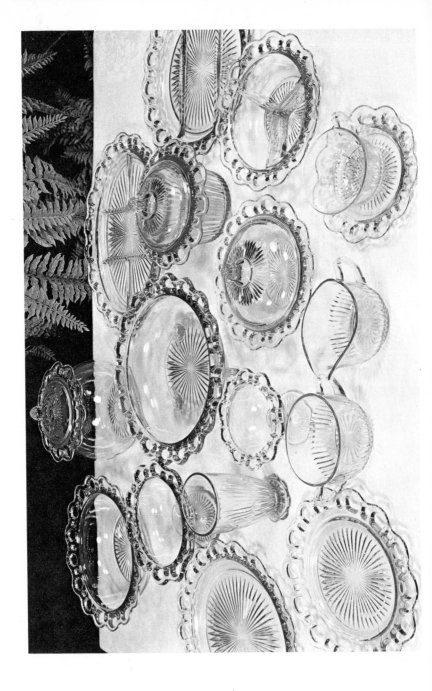

Lace Edge

"Open Lace"; Hocking Glass Co., 1935-1938; table settings in pink; pieces in crystal, "satin finish," orchid decoration; pressed pattern

Hocking's popular pink pattern was first issued in complete table services in 1935 under the official **Lace Edge** name. The pattern has caused its share of confusion. The cups, sugars, creamers, and footed tumblers are often overlooked since they appear at first glance not to be of this set (note picture carefully). Examine, too, the shape of the candlestick, as this is the only one which rightly belongs to Hocking's **Lace Edge**. With the 13" console bowl, the candlesticks make up a "console set."

The Lancaster Glass Company of Lancaster, Ohio, made pink and green pieces in a lace-edged pattern very similar to Hocking's. The sandwich server and candlesticks pictured on page 196 is an example of this company's ware. Imperial and Westmoreland Glass Companies made beautiful lace-edged patterns also.

Most of the bowls are plain, though some are ribbed. The 8" covered bowl might be used as a butterdish, but is actually listed as a "preserve" or "bon bon" and cover. The 4" candy jar without cover was designed so it could be used as a vase with the addition of a crystal frog which one could buy with the set. After the **Lace Edge** line was discontinued in pink, the company (which had become Anchor Hocking) listed the crystal cookie jar, without the cover of course, as a "fish bowl."

A very few pieces were made in crystal, but you may well find

pieces in pink "Satin Finish," Hocking's frosted version of the period glassware. Known pieces of this finish are starred below. The pattern was never reissued in pink, but Anchor Hocking did bring out a line of **Lace Edge** in white glass in the late 1950's which is still being manufactured today. Other companies made similar styles in white glass, too, and in colors as well.

LACE EDGE LISTING

Plate, 10½" dinner
Plate, 10½" grill
Plate, 8½" salad
Plate, 7¼" sherbet or bread and butter
Plate, 10½" round, 3-partitioned, relish
Cup
Saucer
Bowl, 7¾" nappy
*Bowl, 9½" nappy
Bowl, 9½" ribbed
*Bowl, 6½" cereal
*Bowl, console, 3-legged
Platter, 13¾"
Platter, relish, 13¾", 5-partition
Sugar
Creamer
Sherbet
Tumbler, 10½ oz., footed, 5"
Relish Dish, 7½", round, deep
Preserve or Bon Bon and Cover, 7¾"
*Cookie Jar and Cover, round, fat, 5" tall
Candy Jar and Cover, 4", round, ribbed
Flower Bowl with crystal block, 4"
*Comport, 7", footed
Comport and Cover, 7", footed
*Candle Holder
*Vase, 7"

*Satin Finish

Lorain

"Basket"; Indiana Glass Co., 1929-1932; table settings in green, yellow, crystal; mold-etched pattern

A-tisket, a-tasket, green and yellow "Basket" was made by Indiana Glass Company 'way back in 1929. It came in crystal, too, and was their first mold-etched pattern. It has the appearance of an older glass, due to its roughness of finish (edges and seams are heavy and rough) and color. The motif was also mold-etched into a white opaque glass with a lace edge (page 216), and recent times have seen an olive-green issue.

Yellow **Lorain** is the one most often found, but regrettably few collections can boast a set in that or any color. The etched embellishment, is, of course, beautifully executed; no doubt many a collector wishes someone would leave a basketful of sweet **Lorain** at his door.

Plate, 9⅜" dinner	Bowl, 9¾" vegetable, oblong
Plate, 8⅜" salad	Bowl, 6" cereal or oatmeal
Plate, 6" sherbet	Platter, 11½"
Plate, 11½" cake	Sugar, footed, 4"
Cup	Creamer, footed, 4"
Saucer	Sherbet
Bowl, 7⅜" deep berry	Tumbler, 9 oz., 4½"
Bowl, 8" deep berry	Relish Dish, 8", 4-part

Lydia Ray

Of unknown manufacture; early Thirties; table settings in green, crystal, dark blue, burgundy; pressed pattern

One may confuse this pattern with "Ribbon" since both are simple in stature and pure of line. **Lydia Ray,** however, comes in such distinctive Hazel Atlas colors as dark blue and "Burgundy," an amethyst hue, as well as in green and crystal.

Not many people can hope to complete a collection of demure **Lydia Ray** in any color, for evidently there was just not enough made. The name and the listing below are drawn from convention since no records of its origin have yet been discovered.

Plate, 8" luncheon
Plate, 6" sherbet
Cup
Saucer
Bowl, 8" nappy
Bowl, 5" nappy
Creamer
Sugar
Tumbler, 5 oz., 3½"
Tumbler, 9 oz., 4"

Tumbler, 13 oz., 5"
Butter Dish and Cover
Salt and Pepper

Madrid

Federal Glass Co., 1932-1938; table settings in amber, green, pink, blue, crystal; pieces in amber (carnival color); mold-etched pattern

Madrid, a name found on a packing crate containing this pattern, has proved to be the official one. A Federal catalog of the early Thirties shows the mold-etched design under that name. According to Federal spokesmen, the **Madrid** molds were made from the "Parrot" pattern molds which had not done well previously (page 130).

The original line was a big one, but still more pieces were added from year to year. Also during the course of production, the popular "Golden Glow" amber color was perfected.

Mold-etched **Madrid** was first introduced in 1932 in "Springtime Green." In 1933 the green line was made again, and for the first time "Golden Glow" was cast. "Golden Glow" then became the popular color, and was the only one carried from then on.

Pink and "Madonna Blue" **Madrid** were tried around 1933, but were never catalogued. The company had difficulty perfecting the blue color and it was soon cancelled. The pink, too, was only briefly in production. However, both colors are collectable (though scarce) today. The molds were also cast in crystal glass, but it is not known just when or how much. Finally, during the period Federal was making iridescent amber "Normandie" (page 125), they fired the carnival color onto the **Madrid** console bowl and candlesticks.

The butterdish and cover, jam dish, hot dish coasters, and

straight-sided salt-and-pepper were of the earlier production, as were the 9" round and 11" flared bowls. The design on the 9" bowl, by the way, is slightly different from that on the other pieces, but it is definitely part of this set. Later, the jello mold, lower sherbet, footed salt-and-pepper, cookie jar, candlesticks, and pitchers were added to the line. There are four styles of pitchers in all: the juice pitcher, which comes in amber only; a square-shaped pitcher; a round-sided pitcher; and a round-sided pitcher with an ice lip.

The large salad bowl was added to the line about 1936 (when featured on a cake plate it is listed as a "salad set"). Also, many water sets were sold. The last catalog showing **Madrid**—a widely-collected pattern—was in 1938. The listing below is official, compiled from several different catalogs.

MADRID LISTING

Plate, 10½" dinner
Plate, 10½" square grill
Plate, 10½" relish
Plate, 9" luncheon
Plate, 7½" salad
Plate, 6" bread and butter
Cup
Saucer
Bowl, 8¼" nappy
Bowl, 5" nappy or dessert
Bowl, 9" fruit
Bowl, 5" cream soup, handled
Bowl, 7" cereal or soup
Bowl, 10" oval vegetable
Bowl, 11" console, flared out
Bowl, 9½" salad, round, deep
Platter, 11½" meat
Sugar and Cover
Creamer
Sherbet, 2 styles
Pitcher, 36 oz. juice jug, 5" Golden Glow only
Pitcher, 60 oz. jug, square, 8"
Pitcher, 80 oz. jug, 8½"
Pitcher, 80 oz. ice lip jug, 8½"
Tumbler, 5 oz. juice, 4"
Tumbler, 9 oz., 4½"
Tumbler, 12 oz., 5½" iced tea, 2 styles
Tumbler, 5 oz., 4", footed
Tumbler, 10 oz., 5¼", footed

Butter Dish and Cover
Cracker Jar and Cover
Jam Dish, 7"
Candlestick, 2"
Salt and Pepper, 3½"; footed, 3½"
Cake Plate, 11½"
Jello Mold, 2" high,
    (previously called Honey Dish)
Hot Dish Coaster, 5"

Manhattan

"Ribbed (Horizontal)"; Anchor Hocking Corporation, 1939-1941; table settings in pink, crystal; pressed pattern

Manhattan proves to be the real name for what we used to call "Ribbed (Horizontal)." It is unfortunate that few collectors can gather a set of this sparkling pink glassware. The cream-and-sugar and dessert dishes seem to be more available, but certain basic and extra pieces are simply not being found in any abundance. Notice the singular salt-and-pepper to this pattern—so little and square.

Crystal **Manhattan**, which is more plentiful, was made in 1940 and 1941. Know, too, that Westmoreland Glass Company made some larger pieces, such as bowls and a sandwich server, in a similar pink and green design in 1929.

Plate, 10¼" dinner
Plate, 8" salad
Plate, 6" sherbet
Plate, 14" sandwich
Plate, 14" relish, 4-partition
Cup
Saucer
Bowl, 7½"; 9"
Bowl, 4½" dessert, handles
Bowl, 5⅜" fruit, handles
Bowl, 9½", footed, fruit, handles

Sugar and Creamer
Sherbet, low
Pitcher, 42 oz. fruit juice jug
Pitcher, 80 oz. ice lip ball jug
Tumbler, 10 oz., footed
Comport, 5¾" stemmed
Salt and Pepper, 2", square
Candlestick, 4¼" double
Lazy Susan, 14", 5 dividers
Ash Tray, 4"; Coaster, 3½"
Vase, 8"

Mayfair

Federal Glass Co., 1934; table settings in amber, crystal; chipped-mold pattern

A jeweler in Columbus, Ohio, designed this elegant pattern which Federal produced under the name **Mayfair**. However, the patent office would not accept this name, since Hocking already had a "Mayfair." At this Federal apparently decided to scrap the whole effort, because the **Mayfair** molds were then redesigned into the "Rosemary" pattern (page 153). Before the patent office's ruling, however, the pattern had been advertised under the **Mayfair** name in one issue of the **Crockery and Glass Journal,** and a small amount sold. A minimum number of pieces comprise the table services as listed below.

Plate, 9½" dinner
Plate, 6¾" salad
Cup
Saucer
Bowl, 10" oval vegetable
Bowl, 6" cereal
Bowl, 5" nappy
Platter, 12" meat
Sugar, 4", footed

Creamer, 4", footed
Tumbler, 9 oz., 4½"

Mayfair

"Open Rose"; Hocking Glass Co., 1931-1936; table settings in pink, blue; pieces in green, crystal, "satin finish"; mold-etched pattern

Our old open rose design may well be the "mostest" in many a collector's book—most popular, most collectable, most variety of pieces, most widely collected . . . you name it. Hocking named it **Mayfair** and produced it continuously for five full years. Starting in 1931, the complete line as listed below—over fifty pieces—was made in "Flamingo" pink. Table services were made in a beautiful blue, but lacking the wine decanter and wine goblets, plain sherbets, and whiskeys. Only the larger, heavier pieces came in green, and few pieces indeed—the divided platter (sometimes with metal rim) is one—were ever made in crystal. This divided platter, by the way, is not listed in any other color.

A spot check of a few of the more intriguing pieces shows a low, thin-blown sherbet which fits into an indented plate; the wine decanter and goblets; the whiskeys; and the sweet-pea vase. These pieces can be considered hard-to-find compared to other period pieces. Interestingly, the bases of the footed tumblers may be plain, rayed, or checked in design.

In Hocking's characteristic manner, selected pieces were specially acid-etched, or given a "Satin Finish." These cloudy pieces—the salt-and-pepper, large and small bowls, candy jar and cookie jar and covers—proved most popular around the holidays. Dainty flower

motifs, such as a lavender orchid adornment, were hand-painted on the frosty ware.

Hundreds of carloads of **Mayfair** were sold in those five years of production, so it is no wonder there is so much available today. Plates and cups-and-saucers are becoming more scarce every day, however, and it will probably be no time at all before **Mayfair** is gone from the shelves.

MAYFAIR LISTING

    Plate, 9½" dinner
    Plate, 9½" grill
    Plate, 8½" luncheon; 6" bread & butter
    Plate, 6½" sherbet, round; 6½", off center indentation
    Cup and Saucer
**Bowl, 7" nappy; 10", handled
    Bowl, 5½" fruit
 *Bowl, 12" fruit, large, flared-out; 11¾", large, flat
    Bowl, 7" covered vegetable (same as butterdish)
    Bowl, 10" covered vegetable
    Bowl, 9½" oval vegetable
    Bowl, 5" cream soup
    Platter, 12" meat
**Sugar and Creamer
    Sherbet, 3¼; 4¾" high stemmed, thin
    Sherbet, 2¼", low, fits on 6½" plate with off-center indentation
    Pitcher, 37 oz. jug, 6"; 60 oz. jug, 8"; 80 oz. jug, 8½"
    Tumbler, 1½ oz. whiskey, 2¼"; 5 oz. fruit, 3½"
    Tumbler, 9 oz. 4"; 13½ oz. 5¼"
    Tumbler, footed, 3 oz. cocktail, 3¼"
    Tumbler, footed, 10 oz. 5½"; 15 oz. 6½"
    Goblet, 3½ oz. cocktail, 4"; 3 oz. wine, 4½"
    Goblet, 9 oz. 5¾"; thin, 9 oz. 7¼"
    Relish Dish, 4-partition, 8¼"
    Celery Dish, oblong, 10"; 2-partition, 10"
    Cake Plate, footed, closed handles, 10"
 *Cake Plate, flat, handled, 12"
    Butter Bowl and Cover, 7" (same as covered vegetable)
**Cookie Jar and Cover, 6" by 7"
**Candy Jar and Cover, footed, 5" by 8½"
**Salt and Pepper
    Decanter and Stopper, 32 oz., 10½" tall
 *Sandwich Server, handle in center, 12"
    Vase, 5½" by 8½" sweet pea, hat-shaped

*Green
**Satin Finish

118

Miss America

Hocking Glass Co., 1933-1936; table settings in pink, crystal, green; pieces in "satin finish"; pressed pattern

Here she is—**Miss America**! Fashioned by Hocking in 1933, the winning pattern is characterized by distinctive shapes and fine points. Since it was revived from an old English Hobnail mold you may hear it called by that name, but original catalogs and labels preserved intact prove the **Miss America** title.

Large, complete sets can be collected in both pink and crystal. The green is relatively scarce. Harder-to-get pieces might be the tall candy dish and cover, the two large fruit bowls, the water pitcher and goblets—and especialy the butterdish. It is interesting that no butterdish is listed in any of Hocking's catalogs of the day, since a pretty pink one is setting in the company's morgue right now, with the **Miss America** banner still intact. I bet there's many a collector who'd like to get his hands on that beauty! Also in the morgue are little 4½" green nappies—there probably aren't many of those around, either.

Many think that the tall candy dish is a "sweetmeat," but old catalogs will set them straight. "Sweetmeat" dishes were made long before our **Miss America** was.

Hocking had to try a little "Satin Finish" on all its models, and **Miss America** was not left out. All in all, the reign of **Miss America** in the Depression era was a triumphant one indeed.

MISS AMERICA LISTING

Plate, 10¼" dinner
Plate, 10¼" grill
Plate, 8½" salad
Plate, 5¾" sherbet
Cup
Saucer
Bowl, 10" oval vegetable
Bowl, 5½" fruit or cereal
Bowl, 4½" nappy
Bowl, 8" deep fruit
Bowl, 8", curved in at top
Platter, 12" meat
*Sugar
*Creamer
Sherbet
Pitcher, 65 oz., 8½"
Pitcher, 65 oz., 8½" ice lip
Tumbler, 5 oz. juice, 3¾"
Tumbler, 10 oz., 4"
Tumbler, 14 oz., 6"
Goblet, 3 oz. wine, 3½"
Goblet, 5½ oz. juice, 4½"
Goblet, 10 oz., 5½"
Relish Dish, 8½", 4-part round
Celery Tray, 10½", oblong
Relish, divided, 12"
Cake plate, 12", footed
Butter Dish and Cover
Candy Jar and Cover, 11¾" tall
Salt and Pepper, 5"
Comport, 5"
Coaster, 5¾"
Tid-Bit Set, 2-tiered, 8½" plate and 10¼" plate, center metal handle

*Satin Finish

ℿℒoderntone

Hazel Atlas Glass Co., 1934-1937; table settings in blue, burgundy; pressed pattern

This pattern, touched with simple beauty, was made primarily in Hazel Atlas's "Deep Blue," or cobalt; and secondarily in what was called "Burgundy" but what is actually an amethyst shade. Sets of this tableware were made in these two colors from 1934 to 1937. Later the mold was used to make an opaque white ware onto which was sometimes fired a bright red, blue or yellow color. **Moderntone** is the official name for this pressed pattern. It is interesting that cobalt **Moderntone**, like cobalt "Royal Lace," was made from the blue tanks of glass which originally were to have been made into Shirley Temple pieces (see story, page 157).

Plate, 10½" cake or sandwich	Platter
Plate, 9" dinner	Sugar
Plate, 7" salad	Creamer
Plate, 6" sherbet	Sherbet
Cup	Salt and Pepper
Saucer	
Bowl, 8" nappy	
Bowl, 6" nappy	
Bowl, 4" nappy	

New Century

Hazel Atlas Glass Co., 1930; table settings in green; pressed pattern

Another of Hazel Atlas's charming little sets—**New Century,** as it is catalogued—this patternless pattern is perfectly simple in clear green. Luckily, collectors can find most of its pieces preserved today. It is very old for the period, having been made and sold for a brief time only in the early 1930's. A complete listing is not available for this pattern, but known pieces are recorded below. You may, of course, find other pieces in **New Century.**

Plate, 8" luncheon
Cup
Saucer
Bowl, 4¾" nappy
Bowl, 5½" nappy
Sugar
Creamer
Sherbet
Cocktail, fruit, footed

"Bouquet and Lattice"; Federal Glass Co., 1933-1939; table settings in pink, amber, "Sunburst" (a carnival color); pieces in green, crystal; mold-etched pattern

Ⅱormandie

Normandie is the official name for this beautifully-wrought, mold-etched design of Federal's. It was not from an old Carnival mold as is widely believed, but was made especially for the new pink mold-etched glassware that was coming in vogue. It fits into Federal's line after "Patrician" and before "Mayfair."

It was first made in 1933 in "Rose Glow" and crystal. A year later a color called "Sunburst" was created by spraying an iridescent amber onto the patterned crystal ware and then firing it on so well that some people today might think it true Carnival glass. Train-carloads of this **Normandie** in "Sunburst" were shipped to the Great Northern Products Company to be used as premiums.

Later the design was issued in "Golden Glow" as well as in pink again, and the water pitcher and glasses and the salt-and-pepper were added to the line. At some point, a very small amount of green and crystal was made.

Plate, 10½" dinner
Plate, 10½" grill
Plate, 9¼" luncheon; 8" salad
Plate, 6" bread and butter
Cup and Saucer
Bowl, 5" nappy; 8½" nappy
Bowl, 9½" oval vegetable

Platter, 12"
Sugar and Creamer
Sherbet
Pitcher, 80 oz. jug, 8" tall
Tumbler, 5 oz., 4"
Tumbler, 9 oz., 4½"; 12 oz., 5"
Salt and Pepper

Number 612

Indiana Glass Co., 1930-1933; table settings in green, yellow; mold-etched pattern

Lovely old **Number 612** still has no better name than this, which denotes its original line number at Indiana Glass. The early Thirties showed it issued in green and "Topaz." Today, the green is found more frequently than is the yellow.

The pattern is odd in that some pieces are thin and dainty while others are thick and heavy.

Number 612 is not common today. It's a shame, too, because the pattern is at once bold and delicate, and would assemble into a commanding service.

Plate, 10⅜" dinner	Bowl, 6½" cereal
Plate, 10⅜" grill	Bowl, 10" oval vegetable
Plate, 8½" salad	Platter, 10¾" meat
Plate, 11¼" sandwich	Sugar
Plate, 6" sherbet	Creamer
Cup	Sherbet
Saucer	Pitcher, ½ gallon jug, 8½"
Bowl, 7½" nappy	Tumbler, 9 oz., footed
Bowl, 9" nappy	Tumbler, 12 oz., footed
Bowl, 4½" berry	Relish Dish, 3 part

Old Cafe   *Hocking Glass Co., table settings in pink, crystal in 1936-1938; pieces in ruby red in 1940; pressed pattern*

Few collectors probably will ever possess a completed dinner set of this most attractive pattern. Hocking made such a small amount of **Old Cafe** in "Rose Pink" that the plates are rarely seen. The 6" handled olive dish (oblong) and the 8" mint tray (round), which sometimes has a metal holder, are more available probably because they were made special order to be used as premiums. The company lists them in a 1938 catalog as occasional pieces in "Rose."

Old Cafe comes in table settings of crystal, and certain pieces of this pattern were made in "Royal Ruby" (page 160).

Plate, 10" dinner
Plate, 6½" bread and butter
Cup
Saucer
Bowl, 9"
Bowl, 5½" nappy
Bowl, 5" nappy
Bowl, 3¾" nappy
Sherbet, low footed

Tumbler, 3" juice
Tumbler, 4"
Olive Dish, 6" oblong
Mint Tray, 8", low, flared-out
Salt and Pepper

Oyster and Pearls

Anchor Hocking Corp., 1938-1940; pieces in pink, crystal, ruby red, opaque white, opaque white with pink, opaque white with green; pressed pattern

Catchy **Oyster and Pearls** is one of the few major patterns in this book that were never made in table settings. Always advertised in occasional pieces, the pattern was cast in several unique color combinations in addition to "Rose" in 1932, crystal in 1939, and "Royal Ruby" in 1940 (page 160). An opaque white was made, which sometimes appears with a "Springtime Green" fired-on interior, and sometimes with a "Dusty Rose" one. These were devised later in the Forties (page 226).

Smaller pieces of the pattern, such as the heart-shaped jelly dish and the 6½" bon bon, were made-to-order for oatmeal-box premiums. A pattern without a name, it has been tagged **Oyster and Pearls** by its collectors.

Plate, 13½" sandwich
Bowl, 10½" fruit or console
Bowl, 6½" bon bon, deep, handled
Bowl, 5¼" heart-shaped, jelly, one-handled
Bowl, 5¼" round, one-handled

Relish, 10¼" oval, divided
Candle holder, 3½"

Parrot

Federal Glass Co., 1932; table settings in green, amber; mold-etched pattern

Since Federal has not been able to uncover any records of this pattern, we will continue to list it as **Parrot**, the name given it by collectors. Older employees at Federal remember the pattern well, and insist that **Parrot** was not its original name, but they can't recall what it was. The story is that one of the company's designers had just returned from a month in the Bahamas when he was pressed to design a new pattern immediately. All he could think of were parrots and palm trees!

However, the pattern was not what Federal wanted and they felt it would not be popular. There was too much clear space which would scratch easily, and they decided that more of an all-over, etched design was needed. Overnight the molds were remade into the "Madrid" pattern, retaining the **Parrot** shapes.

As explained by Federal spokesmen, the birded pattern was not in production long enough to promote in catalogs. Predominately a green pattern, some light amber was made; also, the color of some green pieces has more of a yellowish-green appearance.

It should be known, too, that Indiana Glass Company made round, thin salad plates in a parrot pattern similar to this square one (page 210).

PARROT LISTING

Plate, 9" dinner
Plate 10½" grill
Plate, 7½" salad
Plate, 6" sherbet
Cup
Saucer
Bowl, 10" oval vegetable
Bowl, 8¼" nappy
Bowl, 5" nappy
Bowl, 7" soup or cereal
Platter, 11"
Sugar and Cover
Creamer
Sherbet
Tumbler, 12 oz., 5½"
Butter Dish and Cover
Jam Dish, 6½'
Salt and Pepper

Patrician   *"Spoke"; Federal Glass Co., 1933-37; table settings in amber, green, pink, crystal; pressed pattern*

The official name for this pattern, previously called "Spoke," is **Patrician**. It was designed and first made in the latter part of 1932 and introduced into Federal's commercial line in January, 1933, in "Golden Glow" (amber) and "Springtime Green." A full line of all pieces was made initially except for the "cream soup" that was added in 1934. A small amount of pink and crystal was issued at some point. By 1935 the catalog listed "Golden Glow" only, and this color was made for two more years. The 10½" dinner plate in "Golden Glow" so commonly found today was made up specially for a large company to use as promotional items.

As is evident in the picture, there is a variety of interesting pieces to watch for such as the hexagonal cookie jar and water pitcher.

The following list was compiled from several old Federal catalogs.

PATRICIAN LISTING

Plate, 10½" dinner
Plate, 10½" grill
Plate, 9" luncheon
Plate, 7½" salad
Plate, 6" bread and butter
Cup
Saucer
Bowl, 8½" nappy
Bowl, 5" nappy
Bowl, 6" cereal
Bowl, 10" oval vegetable
Bowl, 6" cream soup
Platter, 11½" meat
Sugar and Cover
Creamer
Sherbet
Pitcher, 60 oz. jug, 8" tall
Pitcher, 80 oz. jug, 8½" tall
Tumbler, 5 oz., 4"
Tumbler, 9 oz., 4½"
Tumbler, 12 oz. iced tea, 5"
Tumbler, 10 oz., blown footed, 5"
Butter Dish and Cover
Cracker or Cookie Jar and Cover
Salt and Pepper
Jam Dish, 6"

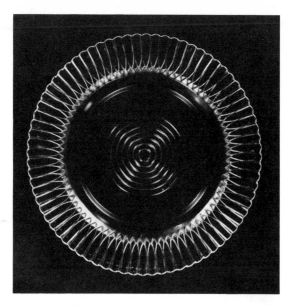

Petalware

"Petal"; Macbeth-Evans, 1930-1936; table settings in pink, crystal, and translucent white; at Corning Glass Works in translucent white with trims until 1940; pressed pattern

Delicate **Petalware** was first made in "Rose Pink" and crystal at the Macbeth-Evans factory in 1930. It is a thin, fragile ware; plates have concentric circles from the center and a fine-scalloped edge. The 12" plate was called a "salver" and no pitcher or tumblers were listed. Few extras, in fact, were made at this time.

In 1932 the pattern was made in Macbeth's new "Monax" tableware, which is a translucent bluish-white. A year later, a cream-colored variation of this, "Cremax," was tried. Some pieces in these two colors have concentric circles, and some do not.

Still later, in 1936, the Macbeth Division of Corning Glass Works (the two companies had merged) experimented with several versions of **Petalware.** They took "Monax" and an ivory color called "Ivrene" and handpainted (1) three pastel bands (pink, blue and green) on it and added a similarly banded crystal tumbler, (2) what they called "Gold Rim **Petalware,**" (3) a gold band with a design in it, or (4) a floral design in bright colors. All these variations were offered in simple table settings as late as 1940, when the **Petalware** molds were finally retired.

Sometimes the pattern is mistakenly thought to be "Fry Glass"

but **Petalware** was made exclusively by Macbeth-Evans. Other companies, of course, may have made similar pressed patterns. At any rate, the clarity and radiance of **Petalware,** especially in the pearly tones, make it a coveted pattern indeed.

PETALWARE LISTING

Plate, 9¼" dinner
Plate, 8" salad
Plate, 6" bread and butter
Plate, 11" salver
Plate, 12" salver
Cup
Saucer
Bowl, 8"
Bowl, 9¼" oval vegetable
Bowl, 5¾" cereal or dessert
Bowl, 4" cream soup, handles
Platter, 13" oval
Sugar
Creamer
Sherbet, 4½", low footed
Salt and Pepper

Pineapple and Floral

Indiana Glass Co., 1932-1937; table settings in crystal, amber; pressed pattern

This is Indiana's #618 pattern, which has no name officially but was described in the May 1933 **Crockery and Glass Journal** as having a "pineapple and floral motif." The 1933 production was in crystal only, and came in luncheon, bridge, and dinner sets as well as open stock. A later issue was made in amber.

Certain pieces of this notable pattern in olive green and milk white are of a recent issue. The listing below is from a 1933 Indiana Glass Company catalog.

Plate, 9⅜" dinner
Plate, 8⅜" salad
Plate, 6" sherbet
Plate, 11½" cake or sandwich
Cup
Saucer
Bowl, 7⅜" deep berry
Bowl, 10" vegetable, oblong
Bowl, 6" oatmeal or cereal
Platter, 11½"

Sugar, diamond-shaped
Creamer, diamond-shaped
Sherbet
Tumbler, 9 oz., 4"
Tumbler, 12 oz., 4½" iced tea
Relish Platter
Comport, 6¼", diamond-shaped
Ash Tray, 4½"

Servitor, 2-tier, 8" plate and 11" plate, metal handle in center
Servitor, 2-tier, 6" plate and 9" plate, metal handle in center

Princess

Hocking Glass Co., 1931-1934; table settings in green, pink, yellow; pieces in "satin finish"; mold-etched pattern

Occasionally one finds preserved on pieces of this finely-executed, mold-etched pattern the label bearing its name, **Princess.** Hocking designed and produced it in 1931. Simple basic sets were made available first in green and then in "Topaz." Later, "Topaz" was dropped from the line and "Flamingo" (pink) added.

Extra pieces such as the cookie jar and cover, large vase, "orange" or "flower bowl" (hat-shaped), and octagonal salad bowl were made in pink and green but not in "Topaz." Sherbets and tumblers are of a thinner glass than other pieces. The base of the footed pieces comes in two designs, checked and rayed. Curiously enough, the mold-etched design is more pronounced on the pieces with the checked figure than on the other.

Princess plates come in several sizes including the grill or divided plate so popular in this period. Notice, too, the variety of tumblers.

Certain pieces of **Princess** were treated with acid to induce what Hocking called its "Satin Finish." The almost-opaque ware was ornamented with hand-painted flower motifs. Satined or not, **Princess** with its nimbus of simple beauty is garnered by many a collector.

PRINCESS LISTING

Plate, 9½" dinner
Plate, 9½" grill
Plate, 11½" handled grill
*Plate, 11½" handled sandwich
Plate, 8" salad
Plate, 6" sherbet (same as saucer)
Cup
Saucer (same as sherbet plate)
Bowl, 9" salad, octagonal
Bowl, 4½" nappy
Bowl, 5½" oatmeal
Bowl, 10" oval vegetable
*Bowl, 9½" orange or flower, hat-shaped
Platter, 12", meat, handled
*Sugar and Cover
*Creamer
Sherbet, thin-blown
Pitcher, 37 oz. jug, 5"
Pitcher, 60 oz. jug, 8"
Tumbler, 5 oz. juice, 3½"
Tumbler, 9 oz., 4"
Tumbler, 12½ oz. iced tea, 5"
Tumbler, footed, 10 oz., 5¼"
Tumbler, footed, 12½ oz. iced tea, 6½"
Relish Dish, 7½", partitioned
Cake stand, footed, 10"
Butter Dish and Cover, 7½"
*Cookie Jar and Cover, 7"
*Candy Jar and Cover, 8½" tall
*Salt and Pepper, 4½"; large 5½"
*Vase, 8" tall
Ash Tray, 4"

*Satin Finish

Queen Mary

Queen Mary was brought into Hocking's line in pink in 1936. You have probably seen the familiar ribbed desserts and cups-and-saucers, but few plates are being found today. A few years later it was made in crystal. Both lines were comprised of full table services and many extras, including the 7¼" round flat candy dish and cover, 10" oblong celery or pickle, and the preserve and cover. The salt shaker illustrated is the one belonging to the set. Not pictured is the 3-section, 12" sandwich and relish plate, or the 4-section, 14" sandwich and relish plate. **Queen Mary**—the official name, by the way—is suprisingly attractive when assembled into sets.

Take care not to confuse Heisey's "Ridgeleigh" line, a vertical ribbed design made in crystal (page 200), with our Hocking's **Queen Mary.**

Plate, 10" dinner

Plate, 8½" salad

Plate, 6" sherbet

Plate, 12" sandwich

Plate, 14" sandwich

Cup

Saucer

Bowl, 7½" nappy

Bowl, 9" fruit

Bowl, 6" fruit

Bowl, 4½" dessert

Bowl, 4" nappy

Bowl, 4" one handle; 5½" two handles

Sugar

Creamer

Sherbet, 5¾ oz., low

Tumbler, 3" juice

Tumbler, 4"

Tumbler, footed, 10 oz., 5"

Preserve Dish and Cover, 7½"

Candy Jar and Cover, 7¼" across, low

Comport, 5¾", footed

Celery or Pickle, 5" by 10"

Salt and Pepper

Relish Plate, 12", 3-partition

Relish Plate, 14", 4-partition

Coaster 3½"

Coaster, Ash Tray, 4¼", square

Ash Tray, 2" by 3¾", oval

Cigarette Jar, 2" by 3", oval

Candlestick, 4½", double

Raindrops

"Optic Design"; Federal Glass Co., 1929-1932; table settings in green; pressed pattern

Most of the pieces belonging to this pattern carry the Federal trademark, the F inside a shield. It is also easily identified by the characteristic inverted dots suggesting its conventional name, **Raindrops.** This pattern is another of Federal's green "Optic Designs."

The following listing is not official, nor is it, in all probability, complete.

Plate, 8" luncheon
Plate, 6"
Cup
Saucer
Bowl, 6" nappy
Sugar
Creamer

Ribbon

Hazel Atlas Glass Co., 1930-1931; table settings in green; pressed pattern

Charming **Ribbon** design is recorded by Hazel Atlas as a nameless green pattern in 1930. It was made a short time only, in luncheon sets with few extras. Notice that the cream-and-sugar resembles those of such other Hazel Atlas patterns as "Cloverleaf" and "New Century."

Ribbon is lovely; it is sad that no more of it is found than is. Its pieces, despite the ultrasimplicity of the lines, are anything but plain when seen in collection.

Plate, 8" luncheon
Plate, 6¼" sherbet
Cup
Saucer
Bowl, 8" nappy
Sugar
Creamer
Tumbler, footed, 10 oz., 5½"
Sherbet
Candy Dish and Cover

Hocking Glass Co., 1927-1932; table settings in green, crystal, crystal with platinum rim; pressed and thin-blown pattern

Ring

Hocking made at least two different green patterns which had **Ring** designs. A very early motif was made in 1927 and called "Circle Design." You can compare it on page 224. Then in 1929, the **Ring** design pictured here was introduced. It is different in shape and with bands of four rings, while "Circle Design" pieces have from four to eight horizontal bands, depending on the piece. **Ring** design comes in green, crystal, and crystal with a platinum rim. A later issue is decorated by black, yellow, and red rings.

As can be seen, a complete set of this pattern would be impressive, due to such a variety of extra pieces as a decanter, a cocktail shaker, and an ice bucket. Below is a 1929 listing of **Ring** design.

Plate, 8" luncheon	Goblet, stemmed, 7"
Plate, 6"	Salt and Pepper, 3"
Plate, sherbet, off-center ring	Decanter and Stopper
Cup and Saucer	Cocktail Shaker
Bowl, 8" nappy; 5" nappy	Ice Bucket, small closed handles
Sugar and Creamer	Sandwich Tray, handle in center

Sherbet, low, fits in sherbet plate
Sherbet, 5" high stemmed
Pitcher, 60 oz., 8" tall
Pitcher, 80 oz., 8½" tall
Tumbler, 5 oz., 9 oz., 12 oz. iced tea
Tumbler, footed cone-shaped, 3" cocktail; 5", 6" iced tea

Rose Cameo

Of unknown manufacture and date; pieces in green; mold-etched pattern

It is probably due to its resemblance to the "Cameo" pattern that this sweet impression is conventionally called **Rose Cameo**. To date, the manufacturer is not known, and so the list below is made up only of those pieces which have come to light so far.

Rose Cameo was made in green, and in a limited number of pieces. The tumblers are found readily enough and can be used to augment other green patterns.

Plate, 7" luncheon
Bowl, 4½" nappy
Bowl, 5" nappy
Cup
Saucer
Sherbet
Tumbler, 6", footed, cone-shaped
Ice Tub, 3" high

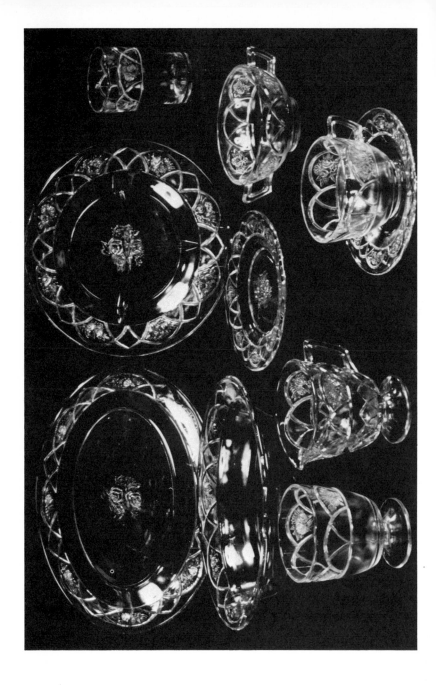

Rosemary

"Dutch Rose"; Federal Glass Co., 1935-1936; table settings in amber, pink, green, crystal; chipped-mold pattern

This pattern, which we used to refer to as "Dutch Rose," is now confirmed to be Federal's **Rosemary**. Patterned from the short-lived "Mayfair" molds (page 113), this design survived little longer and was discontinued in 1936.

Rosemary was offered in simple 4-place table services in "Golden Glow," its most prevalent color today; and in "Rose Glow" and "Springtime Green." Very little is found of these latter colors.

Notice that **Rosemary's** sugar bowl is without a lid or handles and therefore resembles a sherbet. This confusion has resulted in collections that boast a set of sugars instead of a set of sherbets! Also, the pattern around the base of the cup varies sometimes.

The last time **Rosemary** was produced was around 1936, and it has never been reissued.

Plate, 9½" dinner
Plate, 9½" grill
Plate, 6¾" salad
Cup
Saucer
Bowl, oval vegetable
Bowl, 6" cereal

Bowl, 5" nappy
Bowl, 5" cream soup
Platter, 12" meat
Sugar, 4", footed
Creamer, 4", footed
Tumbler, 9 oz., 4¼" tall

Roulette

Hocking Glass Co., 1936-1938; table settings in green; pieces in pink; pressed pattern

Perhaps the roulette wheel—which the dinner plate might be said to resemble—was the inspiration for the conventional name of this pattern, which was advertised in an early Hocking brochure as a "Winning Pattern" indeed. It was considered a promotional line and made in green luncheon sets only in 1936. The service included a pitcher, tumblers, and fruit bowl. There was no cream-and-sugar. The green color is the same yellowish-green as Hocking's "Colonial" pattern, but in a thinner glass which makes it appear even lighter. Some pink was made at one point, but you won't see much of that today. The design was discontinued in 1937.

Plate, 8½" luncheon
Plate, 6" sherbet
Cup
Saucer
Bowl, 9" fruit
Sherbet
Pitcher, 64 oz., 8"
Tumbler, 1½ oz. whiskey, 2½"
Tumbler, 7½ oz. old fashioned, 3¼"

Tumbler, 5 oz. fruit juice, 3½"
Tumbler, 9 oz. table, 4"
Tumbler, 12 oz. iced tea, 5"
Tumbler, 10 oz., footed, 5½"

ℛound ℛobin

Of unknown origin; pieces in green; pressed pattern

Round Robin—as this pattern is conventionally called—is probably one of the many green "optic" pressed designs produced by several different companies in the late Twenties. However, the style of the cup is unique—it is footed!

Listed below are known pieces of this promising pattern.

Plate, 8" luncheon   Bowl, 4" nappy
Plate, 6" sherbet   Sugar
Cup   Creamer
Saucer

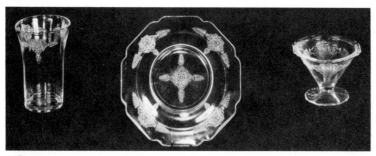

ℛoxana

Of unknown origin; pieces in yellow; mold-etched pattern

There must be more to this pattern than the three pieces shown here, yet these are the only ones I have seen. Its original name and creator are mysteries, too. Christened **Roxana**, the comely pattern can be found in pieces of yellow tableware.

Plate, 6" Sherbet
Sherbet
Tumbler, 9 oz., 4"

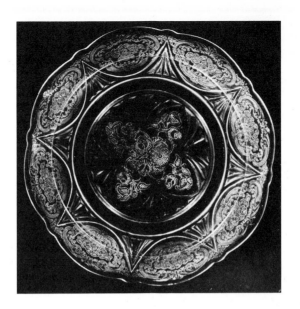

Royal Lace

Hazel Atlas Glass Co., 1934-1941; table settings in pink, green, deep blue, crystal, burgundy; mold-etched pattern

The showy **Royal Lace** is a production in itself. As performed through the years by the famous Hazel Atlas Company, it was a box-office hit when it was first released in 1934. The panoramic settings —pink, green, and crystal, initially—changed with show dates, and three of the original principals—the pitcher, console bowl, and candlesticks—were replaced by newer models; but the show always went on, its story the same:

In 1936 a little-known glass company began to make for a famous corporation a certain line of dark-blue glassware with a special decal. Little did General Mills know when it suddenly cancelled that order that the blue Shirley Temple pieces would cause such a commotion nearly forty years later! Meanwhile, back at the glass works, officials found themselves left with huge tanks of molten blue glass on their hands. Looking over their shoulders in the gloomy morgue, they suddenly espied the **Royal Lace** skeleton molds . . . and there you have the blue **Royal Lace** Story, produced in Techni-cobalt, as told to Hazel Marie Weatherman by an actual on-the-scene employee of Hazel Atlas, and starring Shirley Temple with a cast of pieces. It received a standing ovation wherever it showed.

Then in 1937, part of the original **Royal Lace** cast got the purple-carpet treatment. At least the cookie jar and ice cream dishes (with

metal bases) were given guest appearances in "Burgundy," an amethyst shade (see stills, page 192). Unfortunately, the production had a limited run and its viewing audience is small today.

All in all, the entire **Royal Lace** production enjoyed a long-term engagement, playing in crystal at the Sears, Roebuck Showroom until 1941.

ROYAL LACE LISTING

Plate, 10" dinner
Plate, 10" grill
Plate, 8½" luncheon
Plate, 7" salad
Plate, 6" sherbet
Cup
Saucer
Bowl, 10"
Bowl, 10" oval vegetable
Bowl, 5" nappy
Bowl, 6" nappy
Bowl, 5" cream soup
Bowl, 10", 3-legged
Bowl, 10", 3-legged, ruffled
Bowl, 10", rolled edge
Platter, 13"
Sugar and Cover
Creamer
Sherbet
Sherbet in metal holder
Pitcher, 80 oz., 8"
Pitcher, 54 oz., 8", straight sides
Tumbler, 5 oz., 3"
Tumbler, 9 oz., 4"
Tumbler, 12 oz., 4¾"
Butter Dish and Cover
Cookie Jar and Cover
Candlesticks, 3 styles
Salt and Pepper
Ash Tray, 3½"

Royal Ruby

Anchor Hocking Glass Co., 1939—; table settings in ruby red; pressed pattern

Hocking's first **Royal Ruby** tableware was made in 1939, featuring the round shapes in dinner sets and many accessory pieces. It was at this time also that certain pieces in such patterns as "Oyster and Pearls," "Old Cafe," "Coronation," and the "Royal" pitcher (right center of picture) and tumblers were cast in red glass. (The pitcher at left center was advertised in a 1939 catalog as Hocking's "Spiral Flute" design.)

The red glass was also used for other assorted pieces—often in combination with crystal, for instance—and for "Roly Poly" tumblers during the Forties. It was not until 1949 that the square-shaped ruby red table services were made. Other companies made pieces in red also, but Hocking made all the red ware discussed here.

Below is a listing made up of Hocking's **Royal Ruby** tableware (round shape).

Plate, 9⅛" dinner
Plate, 7¾" salad
Plate, 6½" sherbet
Cup
Saucer
Bowl 8½"
Bowl, 7½" soup
Bowl, 4¼" nappy
Sugar, two styles
Creamer, two styles
Sherbet, 6½ oz.
Pitcher, 42 oz. ball, round
Pitcher, 3 quart, round
Tumbler, 3½ oz. cocktail
Tumbler, 5 oz. juice
Tumbler, 10 oz.
Tumbler, 2½ oz., footed wine
Tumbler, 15-hour candle, 2"
Vase, 4" ivy ball
Vase, 6⅜"

"S" Pattern

Macbeth-Evans Glass Co., 1930-1932; table settings in pink, topaz, crystal, crystal with gold band, crystal with blue band, crystal with platinum rim; mold-etched pattern

This pattern is wanting a name, but since Macbeth lists it as simply the **S-Pattern**, and since the **Crockery and Glass Journal** notes it as **S-Pattern**, and since Macbeth employees knew it and called it simply the **S-Pattern**, I suppose it is only right to record it as **S-Pattern** here. I'd like to call it "Lady Macbeth" but the implications are not the best. At any rate, the pattern was made in "Rose Pink," but more often it is found in crystal and crystal variations, as listed above. A little was made in "Topaz," a yellow gold.

However, comparatively little of it is found at all today, since it was discontinued early and never reissued. Pitchers to the set were made in two styles, one of which is shown.

Plate, 10½" grill	Sugar, 2½", thin; 3", thick, footed
Plate, 8" luncheon	Creamer, 2¾", thin; 3", thick, footed
Plate, 6" bread and butter	Sherbet, thin, low footed
Cup	Pitcher, 80 oz., 7½"
Saucer	Tumbler, 5 oz. juice
Bowl, 8½"	Tumbler, 9 oz.
Bowl, 5½" dessert or cereal	Cake Plate, 11"

Sandwich Design

Our concern in this book is with Depression-era **Sandwich** Design. Little that can properly be termed **Sandwich** Design was made in colors during the period, yet many questions have been raised about it. Perhaps this will clear up some of the confusion:

Anchor Hocking machine-made berry sets in 1939 in pink. In the 1940's it produced a full line of the pattern in crystal. Still later, in the 1950's, certain dark green pieces were created for a cereal company to use as premiums. The late 1950's saw a brief white glass issue. Sometime between 1961 and 1963, **Sandwich** "Desert Gold" was made in a complete line, thus ending Anchor Hocking's involvement with the **Sandwich** pattern. It is interesting that they first called the line "Cape Cod" but later changed it to **Sandwich** Design.

Indiana Glass Company made by hand a full line of their **Sandwich** cut in crystal in the 1920's. The Thirties brought an issue in pink, green, and amber, made in such pieces as plates, candlesticks (tall and short), and console bowls. Then, for the Chicago World's Fair in 1933, Indiana made special ruby red nappies in various sizes. A blue-green version was tried sometime later. Today, the company is still making brilliant, handmade **Sandwich** pattern in crystal and selling it in open stock .

Duncan Miller Glass Company made some pink and a full crystal line of what it called Early American **Sandwich** Pattern in the 1930's.

Westmoreland Glass Company made "Princess Feather," a **Sandwich** design, in complete sets of crystal and some pink and green in 1930, and a "Golden Sunset" (amber) line in 1961.

ANCHOR HOCKING'S **SANDWICH**:

Listing from a 1940 catalog (crystal)

Plate, 9" dinner
Plate, 7" dessert
Plate, 12" serving
Snack Plate and Punch Cup, 9"
Cup
Saucer
Bowls, set of serving, 6", 7", 8"
Bowl, 3-quart salad or punch
Bowl, 6½" serving or salad
Bowl, 8½" relish or vegetable
*Bowl, 8" berry, 4⅞" dessert

Pink

165

Sugar and Cover
Creamer
Sherbet
Pitcher, 2-quart ice lip
Tumbler, 5 oz.; 9 oz.
Tumbler, footed, 9½ oz.
Butter or Preserve and Cover
Cookie Jar and Cover, 9½"

INDIANA'S **SANDWICH:**
Listing from a 1930 catalog (crystal)

Plate, 10½" dinner
Plate, 8⅜" salad
Plate, 6" sherbet; 7" bread and butter
Plate, 8" oval dessert and sherbet
Plate, 13" cake tray
Cup and Saucer
Bowl, 8½" berry; 4¼" berry
Bowl, 6" deep nappy; 6" hexagon nappy
Sugar and Cover
Creamer
Diamond Sugar and Creamer and Tray
Sherbet
Pitcher, 68 oz. jug
Tumbler, footed, 3 oz. cocktail
Tumbler, footed, 8 oz.; 12 oz.
Goblet, 9 oz.
Covered Butter
Sandwich Server, 11", center handle
Celery Tray, 10½"
Console Bowl, rolled edge
Console Bowl, 9", plain; 10" ruffled
Mayonnaise Bowl and Ladle
Puff Box and Cover
Cruet, 6 oz. oil
Wine Bottle, Wine Goblets and Round Tray
Candlestick, low 3½"; tall 8"
Ash Trays, club, diamond, heart and spade

Sharon

"Cabbage Rose"; Federal Glass Co., 1935-1939; table settings in pink, amber, green; pieces in crystal; chipped-mold pattern

Sharon is the official name for this widely-collected pattern, once called "Cabbage Rose." It was made by Federal's new "chipped mold process," a method of production which had been devised after the mold-etched technique, and introduced as "**Sharon** tableware" in 1935. Whole sets of "Golden Glow" (amber) and "Rose Glow" (pink) have been preserved, but to assemble a set in "Springtime Green" is more of a challenge. Few items were issued in crystal; the cake stand is the most often-found crystal piece today.

The footed tumblers which are relatively scarce now were not part of the original set but were added to the line around 1937. A cheese dish and cover appeared in one catalog only, and was sold to cheese companies as a promotional item. This piece is rare today. The sugar bowl sold with or without a cover. The pitcher was made in two styles, plain and ice-lipped.

Sharon was last produced in 1939, and the pattern has never been reissued. Many people, it seems, begin collecting Depression-era Glassware with a first piece of this pattern. I can remember when I got my first piece of **Sharon.** I was 14 years old, and my brother and I won it while pitching pennies at a little county fair in rural Missouri. It was the only piece of this kind of glassware my family

ever had—we couldn't even afford Depression Glass during the Depression! It was not, of course, until thirty years later that I started collecting it seriously.

SHARON LISTING

Plate, 9¼" dinner
Plate, 7½" salad
Plate, 6" bread and butter
Cup
Saucer
Bowl, 8½" nappy
Bowl, 5" nappy
Bowl, 6" soup or cereal
Bowl, 10½" fruit
Bowl, 9½" oval vegetable
Bowl, 7½" soup
Bowl, 5" cream soup, handled
Platter, 12½" meat
Sugar and Cover
Creamer
Sherbet
Pitcher, 80 oz. jug, 9" tall
Pitcher, 80 oz. jug, 9" tall, ice lip
Tumbler, 9 oz., thin blown 4"; 9 oz., thick 4"
Tumbler, 12 oz., thin blown 5¼"; 12 oz., thick 5¼"
Tumbler, 15 oz., footed, cone-shaped 6½"
Cake Plate, 11½", footed
Butter Dish and Cover
Candy Jar and Cover, cone-shaped, 8" tall
Salt and Pepper, flat lids, 2½" tall
Cheese Dish and Cover, domed cover (same as butter), flat
  bottom, 7¼" x ¾"

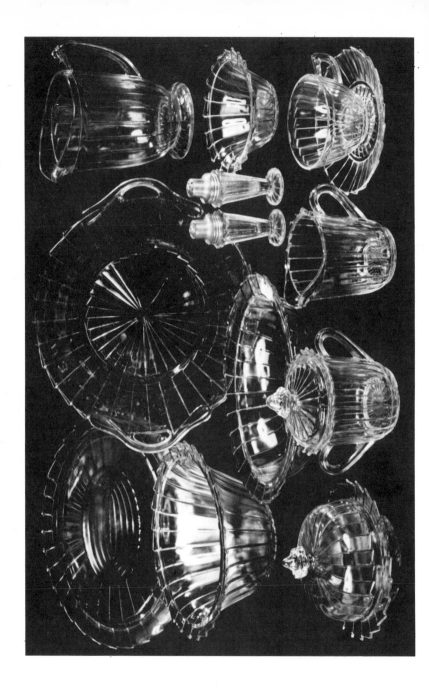

Sierra

"Pinwheel"; Jeannette Glass Co., 1931-1932; table settings in pink, green; pressed pattern

Sierra, what we formerly called "Pinwheel," enjoyed a short production life at the Jeannette factory because it was soon discovered that the serrated edges chipped easily. The pattern is collectable in pink or green tableware; extra pieces—especially the pitcher—are hard to find. The light-hearted pattern was made early in Jeannette's history of Depression glassware, and the mold was never reissued.

Plate, 9" dinner
Plate, 6" sherbet
Cup
Saucer
Bowl, 8½"
Bowl, 9½" oval vegetable
Bowl, 4" nappy
Bowl, 5½" nappy'
Platter, 11"
Sugar and Cover
Creamer
Pitcher, 32 oz. jug, 6½"

Butter Dish and Cover
Salt and Pepper
Sandwich Tray, 10", handled

Spiral

Hocking Glass Co., 1928-1929; table settings in green; pressed pattern

Those green swirl plates and cups you've been seeing probably belong to Hocking's **Spiral** pattern, the name of which is official. It is one of the oldest patterns of the Depression era, and was made into luncheon and dinner sets. Some interesting extra pieces are available in this set if you're lucky enough to come across them in your collecting. Old catalogs show a syrup pitcher and a small, one-handled mixing bowl with spout, which comprise a "waffle set." The sandwich server with center handle is a distinctive piece. The pitcher and tumblers to **Spiral** are of a thinner glass. Also, the original cream-and-sugar have straight sides, while the later ones were footed.

Plate, 8" luncheon
Plate, 6" sherbet
Cup
Saucer
Bowl, 8" nappy
Bowl, 4¾" nappy
Sugar, 2½"; 3"
Creamer, 2½"; 3"
Sherbet

Pitcher, 58 oz. jug, 7½"
Tumbler, 9 oz., 5"
Tray, 9½" sandwich, center handle
Mixing Bowl, 7"
Ice Bucket

Starlight

Hazel Atlas, 1938; table settings in pink, crystal; pressed pattern

The source of **Starlight** was the Hazel Atlas Company, who so aptly named it and listed it in crystal only in an early catalog. Today a number of pink pieces are being found, so the factory apparently experimented with it in this color, also.

Known pieces are listed below. Of course, you may find others—and I wouldn't be too surprised to hear of other colors showing up as well.

Plate, 9" dinner
Plate, 8½" luncheon
Plate, 6"
Plate, 13" cake or sandwich
Cup
Saucer
Bowl, 8½"
Bowl, 5½" cereal
Bowl, 11½" salad
Sugar
Creamer
Salt and Pepper

Strawberry

Of unknown manufacture and date; table settings in crystal, pink, green, light amber (carnival color); mold-etched pattern

It is hoped that plucky little **Strawberry** will show up in an old catalog someday and tell us who it really is. To date, it has been collected in pink, green, crystal, and a light amber which is like a carnival color. Also, a similar pattern with the same mold-shape and rim design has been found—with a cherry instead of a strawberry (see bowl and sherbet on left). **Strawberry** is, of course, a conventional name only.

Plate, 7½" salad
Plate, 6" sherbet
Bowl, 4" berry
Bowl, 6½" deep salad
Bowl, 7½" deep berry
Sugar
Creamer
Sugar and Cover, large, 5½"
Creamer, large, 4⅝"
Sherbet
Tumbler, 9 oz, 3½"

Olive Dish, 5", one-handled
Pickle Dish, 8¼" oval
Comport, 5¾"
Butter Dish and Cover, 7"

Sunflower

Of unknown manufacture and date; table settings in pink, green; mold-etched pattern

It is often thought that only cake plates come in **Sunflower,** since this is the piece usually seen, but actually charming little luncheon sets can be assembled. No doubt the cake plate was made as a promotional item which would explain its prevalence today. Interestingly, the piece varies somewhat in color (the green is often a dark green) and style. **Sunflower** is, of course, only the popular name for the motif.

Plate, 9" dinner
Cup
Saucer
Bowl, 8"
Bowl, 5" cereal
Sugar
Creamer
Tumbler, 8 oz., 5", footed
Cake Plate, 10"
Ash Tray, 5", center design only

Swirl

Jeannette Glass Co., 1937-1938; table settings in pink, opaque blue, and dark blue-green; pressed pattern

The official name for this pattern is **Swirl,** and Jeannette made it for the first time in their greenish-blue, "Ultra-marine," in 1937. The next year, the last it was ever offered, listed it in pink. "Delfite" **Swirl** came out the same year as "Delfite" in "Cherry Blossom"— 1937—but only a small amount was made. It should be noted that the pink is of a slightly different tint than most other sets of this period.

Oddly enough, the butterdish is not listed in "Ultra-marine," although I have seen it in this color, and the salt-and-pepper is not listed in pink. The "Ultra-marine" vase is 8½", while the pink one is 6½". There are tumblers in both colors—a plain one and a footed one, both 9 oz.—but not a pitcher. Candlesticks came in both colors, but the 10½" console is in "Ultra-marine" only. The candy dish and lid was made in both colors.

On the whole, there seems to be more "Ultra-marine" than either pink or "Delfite." **Swirl** may prove to be a hard pattern to collect, but a complete set is an arresting one indeed. The pattern can be recognized by its characteristic border swirls and circles concentric from the center.

Plate, 9¼" dinner
Plate, 8" salad
Plate, 6½" sherbet
Plate, 12½"
Cup and Saucer
Bowl, 9" nappy
Bowl, 5¼" nappy
Bowl, 10½" console, footed
Bowl, 10" fruit, footed, handles
Sugar
Creamer
Sherbet, low footed
Tumbler, 9 oz., 4"
Tumbler, 9 oz., footed, 4½"
Tumbler, 12½ oz.
Candy Dish, 5½", 3-legged
Candy Dish and Cover
Candlestick, double
Butter Dish and Cover
Vase, 6½"
Vase, 8½"
Ash Tray, 5⅜"
Lug soup
Salt and Pepper, 3" fat, polished dome aluminum caps

Tea Room

Indiana Glass Co., 1927-1931; table settings in pink, green, crystal; pressed pattern

No wonder this gigantic line was introduced as "**Tea Room** and Fountain Service" by Indiana Glass Company in 1926—it has obviously been designed for use in the restaurants and soda-fountains of the day. Look at the array of pieces listed!

It is the cream-and-sugar which are found most often today. **Tea Room** predated the mold-etched patterns by a few years, but it came in the colors which were to become the vogue of the next decade—pink, green, and crystal. The glass itself is made to be durable; it is very heavy. Curiously, little of this pattern seems to have been preserved.

Plate, 8¼"
Plate, 6½"
Plate, 10½"
Cup and Saucer
Bowl, 8½" deep berry
Bowl, 9½" deep oval
Bowl, 7½" footed, flat, banana split
Bowl, finger
Bowl, 8½" pickle
Sugar, 3½"
Creamer, 4"
Sugar and Creamer, 4", on handled tray
Sugar and Creamer, oval, on one handle tray
Sherbet, footed, ice cream
Sherbet, low-footed sundae
Sherbet, tall-footed sundae
Sherbet, 6" glace, ruffled as shown in picture
Pitcher, ½ gallon jug
Tumbler, 8½ oz., table
Tumbler, footed, 6 oz. coca cola
Tumbler, 11 oz. iced tea
Tumbler, 12 oz. malted milk
Goblet, 9 oz.
Relish Dish, 2-part bowl
Sandwich Tray, 10½", center handle
Candlestick, low
Salt and Pepper
Ice Bucket
Covered Mustard, plain or slotted cover
Covered Sugar, plain or slotted cover
Parfait
Vase, 11"

Thistle

Macbeth-Evans Glass Co., early Thirties; table settings in pink, green; mold-etched pattern

Little is known about this pattern. Macbeth-Evans employees confirmed it as one of their patterns, and an early one at that, but no records show it at any time. Spokesmen for the company did say it was known as **Thistle** and was not a successful line, so was shortly discontinued. The pieces which have turned up so far are the same shapes exactly as the "Dogwood" molds. Many people no doubt wish there had been more made of this catchy **Thistle**, since to complete a set today could be a thorny problem indeed.

Plate, 9¼"
Plate, 10½" grill
Plate, 8" luncheon
Plate, 6" bread and butter
Cup
Saucer
Bowl, 8½"
Bowl, 9½"
Bowl, 5½", cereal or dessert
Sugar

Creamer
Sherbet, low footed

Thumbprint

"Pear Optic"; Federal Glass Co., 1929; table settings in green; pressed pattern

This pattern is confusing since other companies made similar designs. Most of the pieces pictured, however, carry the Federal trademark and appear in an early catalog of that company where they are described as having a "Pear Optic" figure. Collectors like to call it **Thumbprint**.

There are several reasons why a table service is so hard to collect today. The line was small, and made only for a short length of time. Cups and saucers were given as premiums, and on the whole the glassware was used so heavily as everyday tableware that few pieces were preserved.

Thumbprint is one of the oldest Depression-era patterns. It appears even before the mold-etched designs.

Plate, 9¼" dinner
Plate, 8" luncheon
Plate, 6" sherbet
Cup
Saucer
Bowl, 8" nappy

Bowl, 5" nappy
Sugar
Creamer
Sherbet
Tumbler, 4"
Salt and Pepper

Twisted Optic

"Swirl #1"; Imperial Glass Co., late Twenties; table settings in two green shades, amber, and pink; pressed pattern

Twisted Optic is a phrase used by Imperial to describe the swirl pattern made by them in the last few years of the Twenties. It was made in "Golden Green," "Imperial Green," amber, and a new shade of pink—"Rose Marie, of rose tint" as they called it. Imperial made many different pieces and patterns in "Rose Marie" color, including the **Twisted Optic** pictured here. The pieces listed below are from a late Twenties catalog.

Plate, 8" luncheon
Plate, 7" salad
Plate, 6" sherbet
Cup
Saucer
Bowl, 8" nappy
Bowl, 5" nappy
Bowl, 12" console, rolled edge
Sugar
Creamer
Sherbet

Pitcher
Tumbler, 4½"
Candy Jar and Cover
Candlestick, 3"
Coaster

Vernon *Indiana Glass Co., 1931; table settings in yellow, green, crystal; mold-etched pattern*

This rare pattern, with its graceful style and meticulous etching, is an early Indiana Glass pattern. It's being called **Vernon**, although it carried no official name in 1931. That little was made, however, is known to be true, and a completed set today would be quite a phenomenon, as well as being phenomenally lovely. The pieces pictured here are in Indiana's characteristic yellow shade, "Topaz," but **Vernon** also comes in green and crystal, as was verified by the company.

Plate, 8" luncheon
Plate, 6" sherbet
Plate, 11" sandwich
Cup
Saucer
Sugar, 4", footed
Creamer, 4", footed
Sherbet
Tumbler, 5", footed
Relish Dish, 7", 3-part

Waterford

"Waffle"; Anchor Hocking Corp., 1938-1944; table settings in pink, crystal; pressed pattern

We once called this distinctive mold the "Waffle" pattern, but production records of the Hocking Division of Anchor Hocking Corporation show it to be **Waterford**, a "Rose Glass Tableware" of 1938. At that time the Thirties' intrigue with colored glassware was waning, and this was one of the company's last patterns to come in pink. The small line was only carried for one year, tapering off to just the berry dishes and occasional pieces of which we see several today. Then in 1939 **Waterford** was introduced in crystal table services, this time with many additional pieces as are listed below. The crystal production lasted through 1944, when a short "war line" offered occasional pieces only.

Plate, 9⅝" dinner
Plate, 7⅛" salad
Plate, 6" sherbet
Plate, 10¼" cake, handled
Plate, 13¾" sandwich
Cup
Saucer
Bowl, 8¼"
Bowl, 5¼" nappy
Bowl, 4¾" dessert
Sugar and Cover
Creamer
Sherbet
*Pitcher, 42 oz. fruit juice jug
Pitcher, 80 oz. ice lip jug
Tumbler, 10 oz., footed, 5"
*Goblet, 6"
Butter Dish and Cover
*Salt and Pepper
*Coaster, 4"
*Ash Tray, 4"
Lazy Susan, 14"

*Crystal only

187

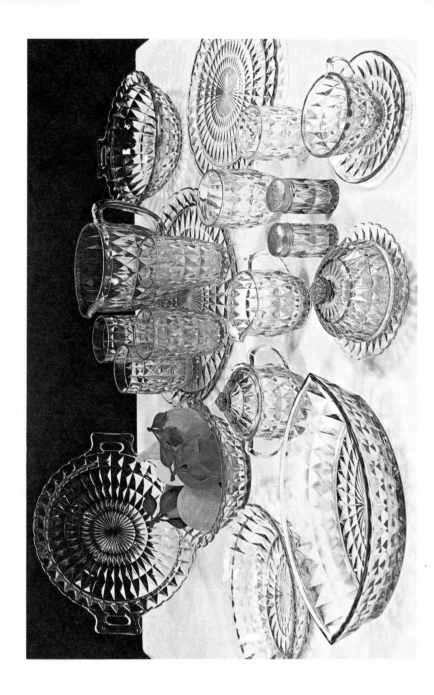

Windsor

*"Windsor Diamond"; Jeannette Glass Co., 1936-1940;
table settings in pink, green, crystal; pressed pattern*

The original advertisements for this diamond design carried a picture of "Windsor Castle—The King's Castle—England," for which the pattern was named. In 1936, dinner sets, refreshment sets, luncheon sets, and occasional pieces were listed in pink and green. A year later, the only two colors catalogued were crystal and "Wild Rose." Remarkable pieces in this set include the pyramid candlesticks, the square relishes, and the heavy, boat-shaped bowl. Even the powder jar and cover and a 10 oz. nappy with a snap cap were a part of the original line.

The last year **Windsor** was listed in pink by Jeannette was 1940, but crystal was offered as late as 1946. It was in this later issue that the footed tumblers, tall compote, and a second style of cream-and-sugar appeared. A few pieces were also made later in white glass.

It should be known that Hocking Glass came out with a water set (pitcher and tumblers only) in 1935 which they called "Windsor," but it is not a part of this set. To end confusion, Hocking soon changed its name to "Royal" (page 223).

Plate, 9" dinner
Plate, 7" salad
Plate, 6" sherbet
Cup
Saucer
Bowl, 4¾" nappy
Bowl, 8½" nappy
Bowl, 5½" deep cereal
Bowl, 9½" oval vegetable
Bowl, 9½" handled
Bowl, 10½" fruit or console
Bowl, 7" x 11¾" fruit, boat-shaped
Bowl, 7", legged
Bowl, cream soup
Bowl, 5⅛" cereal
Platter, 11½"
Sugar and Cover, second style crystal only
Creamer, second style crystal only
Sherbet
Pitcher, 52 oz. jug, juice, 5"
Tumbler, 5 oz., 3"
Tumbler, 9 oz., 4"
Tumbler, 12 oz., 5"
Tumbler, footed, 7", crystal only
Relish Platter, 11½"
Cake Plate
Butter Dish and Cover
Candy Dish and Cover, low, cheese or jam
Candlestick, 3"
Salt and Pepper
Chop Plate, 13⅝"
Sandwich Tray, 10¼", handles
Tray, 15½"
Square Tray, 4"
Tray, oblong, 4⅛" x 9"
Tray, oblong, 8½" x 9¾"
Ash Tray, 5¾"
Coaster, 3"
Powder Jar and Cover
Nappy, 10 oz., with sterling seal and snap cap

LEFT TO RIGHT, TOP TO BOTTOM: 1. Cigarette Holder; Ash Trays; Cream and Sugar, vertical ribbed, in dark blue also 2. Salt and Pepper, 5½'', etched design 3. Condiment Set by Imperial Glass Co. 4. Vase, 7'', etched design (two girl figures) 5. Bonbon, 6½'' 6. Swan, 2½'' 7. AMERICAN SWEETHEART Salver, 12''. Macbeth-Evans Glass Co. 8. Plate, 7½'' 9. EARLY AMERICAN SANDWICH Candlestick, 8''. Indiana Glass Co. 10. Ice Bucket, 6'' 11. ROYAL LACE Cookie Jar, Hazel Atlas Glass Co. 12. BLOCK Jug, 56 oz. 13. Jug, 56 oz.; Tumbler, 9 oz. 14 STAG AND HOLLY Bowl, 11'' (also made in two other styles) 15. Celery Dish, 9'', marked ⚔, Cambridge Glass Co. 16. Individual Salts 17. Handled Nappy, 5'', marked ◇, Heisey Glass Co. 18. Goblet, basket design 19. Fruit Bowl, 11'' PIONEER line, Federal Glass Co. 20. Bud Vase 21. Shirley Temple Pieces 22. Candy Dish in metal holder, 8'' 23. Bowl with bird handles, 7½'' 24. Console Set, 3-piece, pink, green, amber, Imperial Glass Co. 25. Berry Sugar, Bartlett-Collins Co. 26. Ash Tray, 3¼'' (was advertised with DOGWOOD), Macbeth-Evans Glass Co. 27. Ash Tray Set, pink, green, amber, and blue, 2'' x 2½''

192

Occasional and Occasionally-Found Pieces

This final chapter has been composed in order to present two categories of Depression Glass not included in the "Major Pattern Discussions" in the body of this book. One category might be called "occasional pieces" and the other "occasionally-found pieces."

"Occasional Pieces" are, of course, what we often call "conversation pieces," or items made and sold not as part of any patterned set but individually. I use the phrase "occasionally-found pieces" to mean those items which are probably part of a patterned set, but are collected to a lesser extent than those seventy-eight major patterns. Because these patterns are scarce, or for some other reason are not being widely collected, I do not have as much information to write about them. So, I simply list the name, manufacturer, date, and colors, as I know them.

Because most of the patterns shown in this chapter were never officially named by their makers, I choose to list them numerically rather than try to garner conventional names for them all. The dates given indicate the years I found them listed—not necessarily the only years they were made and sold.

To attempt to represent **all** of the Depression Glass patterns is to dream the impossible dream. My solution to the problem is to exemplify rather than to exhaust. For instance, there are many companies other than the ones previously discussed which made the colored glass during the Depression years. In this section I try to give at least an example of some of these companies' wares.

One of these, for instance, is the Bartlett-Collins Company in Sapulpla, Oklahoma, who did not make table services in pink and green but did make several lines of occasional pieces in the Thirties.

Also included in this section are examples of the thin, crystal-like etched colored ware; the opaque dinnerware; and the pink and green kitchenware—all of which were made during the period.

You will notice too that I have shown a few items which are not Depression Glass. That is because these items have been questioned so many times by collectors that it only makes sense to end the confusion where possible.

28. SUNKIST Reamer, 6", pink, green, milk white, "Sunkist" inscribed on side, "Made in U. S. A. Patent No 68764" inscribed on base

29. SUNKIST Orange Bowl, 7" high and 12" across, pink, green, "Sunkist" inscribed on base

30. MISSION Juice Dispenser, 8" high, pink, green, "Mission" inscribed on side

31. Basket, 9½" tall including handle, pink, green, early Thirties, later in blue, amber, crystal, Bartlett-Collins Co.

32. Plate, 7¾"; Handled Nappy, 5½"; pink, amber, blue, and crystal, early Thirties

33. Salad Plate, 8", pink ("Rose Marie"), green, amber, late Twenties, early Thirties, Imperial Glass Co. (only piece shown in this pattern)

34. DIAMOND BLOCK, raised pattern, 8" Celery Tray; 4¾" Handled Olive Dish; 6½" Handled Pickle Dish; pink, green, crystal, late Twenties, early Thirties, additional pieces available: 4" Footed Jelly Dish (comport); 8½" Celery Tray, square shape; 7" Berry Bowl; 4½" Berry Dish; 3" Sugar; 3½" Creamer; 7" Nappy; 5½" Nappy; 5½" Creamer; 6" Pitcher; 5½" Square Nappy

35. DIAMOND design, Candlesticks, 3½", advertised in 1930 with 10½" Console Bowl, rolled edge, pink, green (not part of Jeannette's WINDSOR tableware)

36. Dish, 7", pink, green, crystal, late Thirties, Anchor Hocking Glass Co.

37. Vase, 12", floral design, pink satin finish, early Thirties

38. Vase, 15", floral design, pink, crystal, late Twenties, Bartlett-Collins Co.

39. Lamp, 31 oz. oil capacity, pink ("Nu-Rose"), green ("Nu-Green"), early Thirties, Bartlett-Collins Co., marked in glass near insert collar "Patented March 17, 1925" (Bartlett-Collins Co. still makes a similar lamp today in many colors)

40. Lamp, 10" tall, rose design, green

196

41. LACED EDGE Sandwich Server, 12"; Candlesticks, 2"; pink, green (also etched, decorated, and satin finished), early Thirties, Lancaster Glass Co., many additional pieces

42. Jug, 42 oz.; Tumbler, 13-oz.; enameled, grape motif, pink, green, crystal, early Thirties, Barltett-Collins Co. (other companies made similar enameled grape designs in pitchers and tumblers)

43. Ice Tub with Handle, pink, green, crystal, late Twenties, Indiana Glass Co., Line #610, made just before our NO. 612 pattern, listing from original catalog: Handled Berry Cream; Handled Berry Sugar; 8 oz. Footed Service Tumbler; 11 oz. Footed Service Tea; Half Gallon Jug; 9¼" Oval Bowl; 9½" Pickle Dish, open handles; 4" Berry Dish; 8½" Berry Bowl; 8½" 4-part Relish Dish, center handle; 3-piece Sugar and Creamer Set (tray has center handle)

44. Etched Ice Bucket, 6" tall, pink, green, late Twenties

45. Nite Set: Jug, 32 oz.; Tumbler, 5 oz; pink, green, crystal, middle Thirties

46. Pitcher, 80 oz.; Tumbler, 5 oz., 9 oz., 12 oz.; etched grape design, pink, green, crystal, middle Thirties, Hocking Glass Co. (you may find other pieces in this line)

47. Cake Plate, 7½", floral pattern, pink, green, crystal, late Twenties

48. Cake Plate, 10" (12" not shown), pink, light green, late Twenties, United States Glass Co. (marked "U S G Co. patent pending")

49. LOMBARDI Bowl, 10½", light blue, late Thirties, Jeannette Glass Co. (a later issue — it measures 9½" across and its ends are straight up — is being made in many colors today)

50. Relish Plate, 13", closed lace edge, pink (also made in satin finish with orchid decoration), middle Thirties, Hocking Glass Co.

51. Cake Plate, 12¾", DIAMOND LATTICE design, pink, green, crystal, early Thirties

52. Cake Plate, 12", WHEAT design, pink, green, crystal, early Thirties

53. DOLPHIN Candlesticks, 4'', pink, green, crystal, late Twenties

54. DOLPHIN Candlesticks, 7½'', pink, green, crystal, late Twenties

NOTE: Westmoreland Glass Co. made a DOLPHIN candlestick similar to Items 53 and 54, but with a hexagon base, in the late Twenties and early Thirties in pink, green, and a light blue. They are still using the mold today for milk glass and crystal.

55. DOLPHIN Bowl, 9'' ruffled, pink, green, amethyst, early Thirties

56. Candlesticks, 3½'', DOLPHIN trim, pink, green, crystal, early Thirties

57. Relish Plate, 10½''; Plate, 7''; 7 oz. Goblet; Creamer; pink, green, crystal, late Twenties, marked ◊ , Heisey Glass Co. (you may find other pieces in this line)

58. Candlestick, 8½'', pink, late Twenties

59. Candy Jar and Cover, 8½'', pink, green, late Twenties

60. Cigarette Holder, 4½'', pink, green, early Thirties

61. Cake or Sandwich Plate, 11'', pink, green, middle Thirties

62. Plate, 7½''; Creamer; pink, green, crystal, early Thirties

63. Mayonnaise Server, 6½'', pink, green, crystal, early Thirties, United States Glass Co. (marked U S G Co., letters intertwined)

64. Bowl, 8½'', pink, green, crystal, middle Thirties

65. Handled Nappy, 5½'', pink, green, crystal, early Thirties

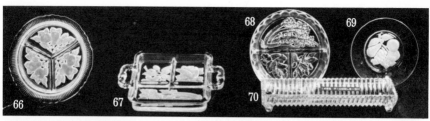

66. INTAGLIO pattern, Relish Dish, 7½", 3-part, assorted fruit, crystal, middle Thirties

67. INTAGLIO pattern, 7" Celery, Olive, or Pickle Dish, 3-part, square, handled, crystal, early Thirties, Indiana Glass Co.

68. Relish Dish, 7½", round, clear crystal with embossed center design of celery, olive, and pickles, late Thirties, Indiana Glass Co.

69. INTAGLIO pattern, 6¼" Plate, fruit design, crystal, late Twenties, Jeannette Glass Co.

70. RIDGELEIGH line, 12" Relish Dish, footed, 2-part, crystal, late Twenties, marked ⊕ , Heisey Glass Co.

71. Plate, 8½"; Nappy, 5"; star center, swirled design, green, pink, crystal, early Thirties

72. Sandwich Server, 10", pink, green, early Thirties (you may find other pieces to match this pattern)

73. Platter, 10½", pink, green, early Thirties (you may find other pieces to match this pattern)

74. Relish, 5", pink, green, middle Thirties, Indiana Glass Co.

75. Relish, 6", pink, green, middle Thirties, Indiana Glass Co.

76. Relish, 7", 4-part; Coaster, 3½"; pink, green, early Thirties, Indiana Glass Co.

77. Mold-etched Bowl, 9½"; Sandwich or Cake Plate, 10¾"; Flat Fruit Bowl, 11½"; pink, green, yellow, middle Thirties, Hocking Glass Co.

78. VERNICULATE pattern, Flower Block, 4"; Candy Dish, 6"; Candlestick, 2½"; pink, green, crystal, early Thirties (you may find other pieces of this pattern)

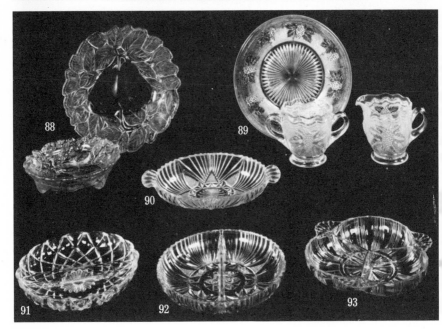

79. Toy Mug, 1 oz., pink, green, crystal, late Thirties, Federal Glass Co.

80. Whiskey Tumbler, 1 oz., pink, green, middle Thirties, Federal Glass Co.

81. Candlestick, 3", pink, green, satin finish, middle Thirties

82. Tray with middle handle, 4" x 9½"; 1 oz. Miniature Tumblers; pink, middle Thirties

83. Individual Salts, pink, oval-shaped

84. Cream and Sugar Set, pressed design, pink, green, crystal, early Thirties

85. EARLY AMERICAN SANDWICH pattern, Goblet, 9 oz., pink, green, crystal, Duncan and Miller Glass Co. (this company also made other pieces in pink and green)

86. Tumbler, 9 oz., pressed design, pink, crystal, middle Thirties, Federal Glass Co.

87. Cream and Sugar, beading and rings, pink, green, crystal, early Thirties

88. AVOCADO pattern (pears and leaves), Salad Plate, 8¼"; Footed Relish, 6"; pink, green, crystal, late Twenties (later made in milk white), Indiana Glass Co., Line #601, additional pieces: 10" Two-handled Plate; 8" Two-handled Pickle; 5¼" Two-handled Olive; 7¼" Shallow Preserve; 6½" Cheese Plate; Footed Tumbler and a ½-Gallon Jug; Cream and Sugar Set

89. Stippled Glassware with grape or berry, 8½" Plate; Cream and Sugar (you may find additional pieces in this pattern)

90. Relish Dish, 8" oblong, pink, green, crystal, late Thirties

91. Relish Dish, 6", two-part, pink, green, crystal, middle Thirties

92. Relish Dish, 6½", two-part, pink, green, crystal, late Thirties

93. Relish Dish, 6½", 3-part, pink, green, crystal, late Twenties

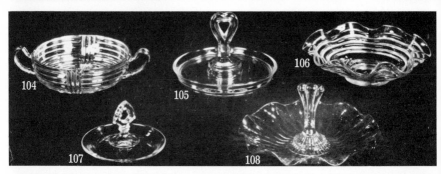

94. Sugar Bowl, ringed design, pink, green, crystal, middle Thirties

95. Handled Plate, 7'', clear pink (more than one company made this style plate)

96. Footed Flat Bowl, 8'', clear light pink

97. Berry Creamer, pink, green, light blue-green, late Twenties and Thirties, Bartlett-Collins Co.

98. Coaster Ash Tray, 4'', ruffled edge, checked bottom, pink, green, amber, crystal, middle Thirties, Federal Glass Co.

99. Coaster, 3¼'', pink, green, amber, middle Thirties, marked Ⓥ Federal Glass Co. (several companies made similar coasters in pink and green)

100. Etched Bowl, 9'', pink, early to middle Thirties

101. Etched Sugar and Creamer, 2½'', pink, Thirties

102. Etched Salt and Pepper, 4'', pink, Thirties

103. Etched Relish Dish, 4½'' x 11'', pink, Thirties

104. Handled Nappy, 6'', pink, crystal, middle to late Thirties, Hocking Glass Co.

105. Bonbon Server, 6'', center handle, pink, green, Thirties

106. Ruffled Nappy, 7½'', pink, green, crystal, middle Thirties

107. Small Server, 4'', pink, green, crystal, Thirties

108. Handled Mint Tray, 7¼'', pink, green, crystal, late Thirties, Hocking Glass Co.

109. Bowl, 8½''; Vase, 8''; Bowl, 10''; pink, crystal, middle Thirties, Hocking Glass Co.

110. Footed Bowl, 11'', 3-legged, flanged rim, floral design, pink, green, black, crystal, Thirties

111. BRIDGE ASH TRAY SET: club, diamond, heart, and spade decoration, pink, early Thirties, Hocking Glass Co.

112. BRIDGE REFRESHMENT SET: club, diamond, heart, and spade decoration, four 13 oz. Tumblers; Tray with center handle; pink, middle Thirties

113. Etched Jug and Cover, 82 oz., pink, early Thirties

114. LIDO Tumbler, footed, 15 oz., pink, green, amber, crystal, early Thirties, Federal Glass Co. (Federal also made 5-oz., 9-oz., and 12-oz. Tumblers, not footed, and a 65-oz. LIDO Jug)

115. LOVEBIRD AND GRAPE design, Tumbler, 9 oz., crystal with green enameled decoration, late Twenties (also available to match is a 64-oz. Jug with stuck handle)

116. MAYFAIR Relish Platter, 12" with metal frame, crystal only, middle Thirties, Hocking Glass Co. (also made without frame)

117. Salt and Pepper Holder, center handle, pink, crystal, early Thirties

118. Cuspidor, AZTEC decoration, iridescent amber, green, early Thirties, Hocking Glass Co.

119. Salt and Pepper, 3½", green, early Thirties, marked ⋈ , Hazel Atlas Glass Co.

120. Salt and Pepper, 2", pink, green, dark green, deep blue, crystal, marked ⋈ , Hazel Atlas Glass Co.

121. Salt and Pepper, 3½", ringed design, pink, green, crystal, early Thirties, marked ⋈ , Hazel Atlas Glass Co.

122. Salt and Pepper, 3½", round, ribbed, Thirties, marked ⋈ , Hazel Atlas Glass Co.

123. Salt and Pepper, 3", 3-sided, pink, light green, early Thirties

124. Salt Shake, 4", metal with green glass bottom, late Twenties

125. Salt Shake, 5½", 8-sided, mold-etched design, green, early Thirties

126. CASTER SET: Salt and Pepper on center-handled Tray, green, early Thirties, Hocking Glass Co.

127. Salt and Pepper, 4", pewter top and handle, pink, late Twenties

128. Salt Shake, 3", green, early Thirties, Bartlett-Collins Co.

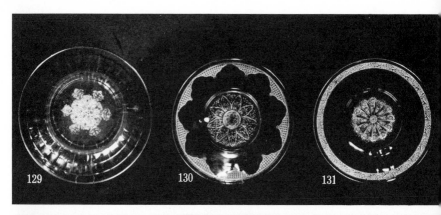

129. SNOWFLAKE Plate, 8½", green, early Thirties

130. CATHEDRAL Plate, 8", pink, green, crystal, early Thirties, Hocking Glass Co.

131. VIRGINIAN Plate, 8", pink, green, early Thirties

132. LEAF pattern, Plate, 8", green, pink, crystal, early Thirties, Macbeth-Evans Glass Co.

133. ROSE ON TRELLIS Plate, pink, early Thirties

134. Octagon Plate, 7", star center, pink, green, crystal, early Thirties

135. Sherbet, paneled, pink, green, crystal, middle Thirties

136. Tumbler, 9 oz., ringed, green, early Thirties, marked ⋈, Hazel Atlas Glass Co.

137. Tumbler, 9 oz., green, early Thirties, Bartlett-Collins Co. (the company also made a 12-oz. iced tea)

138. Tumbler, 9 oz., etched design, yellow

139. BERRY SET (ruffled edges): Bowl, 8½"; Nappy, 4½"; pink, green, deep blue, burgundy, crystal, Thirties, Hazel Atlas Glass Co.

140. BERRY SET: Bowl, 8"; Nappy, 4"; pink, green, deep blue, burgundy, crystal, Thirties, Hazel Atlas Glass Co.

141. DIAMOND OPTIC Berry Set: Bowl, 8"; Nappy 4½"; pink, crystal, middle Thirties, Hocking Glass Co.

142. BLOCK PANEL design, Bowl, 7½"; Nappy, 4½"; green, pink, late Twenties, early Thirties

143   144   145

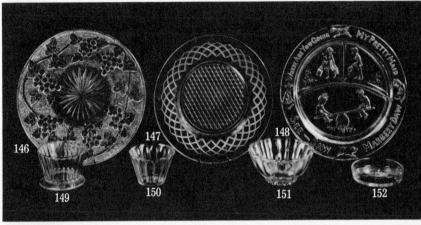

146   147   148

149   150   151   152

153   154

143. PARROT design, Thin Salad Plate, 8½", green, 1930, Indiana Glass Co.

144. BERRY design, Thin Salad Plate, 8½", green, 1930, Indiana Glass Co.

145. FRUIT design, Thin Salad Plate, 8½", green, 1930, Indiana Glass Co.

NOTE: Also included in this series by Indiana Glass Co. was an 8 1/2" "NO. 612" thin salad plate.

146. GRAPE design, Salad Plate, 8", heavy, stippled, pink, green, early Thirties

147. DIAMOND LATTICE design, Plate, 7½", pieces in pink, green, amber, crystal, early Thirties, Federal Glass Co.

148. Child's Plate, 8", with "Where Are You Going My Pretty Maid" and "See-Saw Margery Daw" inscribed, pink, green, crystal

149. Fruit Cup, 3", footed, green, middle Thirties

150. Custard Cup, 2½", green, marked ▯, Hazel Atlas Glass Co.

151. Berry Dish, 4½" (not shown: berry bowl, 7¼"), green, amber, Federal Glass Co.

152. Coaster, 3", green, early Thirties, marked ▯, Hazel Atlas Glass Co.

153. Tableware in crystal (some occasional pieces have fruit motif in the center), Pattern #622, middle Thirties, Indiana Glass Co., pieces available: 9⅜" Dinner Plate; 8⅜" Salad Plate; 6" Plate; 11½" Sandwich or Cake Plate; 7½" Coupe Soup; 9" Berry Bowl; Cup and Saucer; Fruit Cup Plate or Cheese Plate (one closed handle); Fruit Cup; 7" Handled Olive; 2-Handled Pickle Dish; 5 oz., 9 oz., 12 oz. Tumblers; 39 oz. Jug (made thru the Fifties)

154. Imitation Crackle, Plate, 8"; Bowl, 5"; Sherbet; pink, green, dark green, amber, crystal, Twenties, Thirties (most all companies made their own "crackle" design)

155. FLORAL AND DIAMOND BAND, Bowl, 8"; Sherbet; Sugar (made with cover), 5¾" tall; Creamer, 4¾"; pink, green, late Twenties (jug, tumblers, and butter dish also available)

156. DIAMOND PANEL pattern, Butter Dish; 6" Plate; Sherbet; Creamer; 9 oz. Tumbler; pink, green, iridescent, late Twenties (you may find other pieces of this line)

157. WHEAT AND STAR Plate, 6½"; Nappy, 4"; crystal, late Thirties, Federal Glass Co., only two pieces listed (don't confuse this pattern with Anchor Hocking's "Laurel Wreath" tableware made in the Fifties in crystal)

158. BARK pattern, Plate, 8"; Ice Tub, 3" high, 6" diameter; pink, green, crystal

159. SCROLL design, Plate, 6"; Sugar; Cup; light green tableware, late Twenties, United States Glass Co. (you may find other pieces of this pattern), "U S G Co." intertwined on some pieces

160. DIAMOND LATTICE design, Bowl, 7"; Nappy, 5½"; Plate, 9¼"; pink, crystal, late Thirties, Federal Glass Co.

161. SUNBURST pattern, tableware in crystal, 1938-1941, Jeannette Glass Co., 9¼" Dinner Plate; 12" Chop Plate; 12" Round Tray; Cup and Saucer; 4¾" Nappy; 8½" Nappy; 9 oz. Tumbler; Cream and Sugar; Sherbet Plate; Oblong Divided Relish Tray

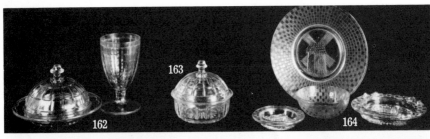

214

NOTE: *Items 162-166 are all marked* 🄷 *, made by Hazel Atlas Glass Co.*

162. BLOCK pattern, Butter Dish; Tumbler, 9 oz.; green, pink, crystal, early Thirties

163. COLONIAL BLOCK pattern, Round Butter Dish and Cover, 4½" in diameter, green, crystal, pink, early Thirties

164. WINDMILL AND CHECKERBOARD design, 8" Plate; 4" Ash Tray; 4", 5½" Nappy; green, crystal, late Twenties, some pieces carry just checkerboard design

165. Cream and Sugar, "X" design in squares, pink, green, crystal, early Thirties

166. COLONIAL BLOCK pattern, Cream and Sugar and Cover, 5"; Candy Jar and Cover, 8½"; Bowl, 7"; pink, green, crystal, early Thirties, milk white later

167. Plate, 6½"; Nappy, 4½", 5½"; Nappy, 4"; Low Footed Sherbet or Custard; green, pink, crystal, early Thirties

168. Tumbler, 9 oz.; Sauce Pitcher on 5" Plate; light green

169. Bowl, 9½"; Plate, 12¼"; pink, crystal, middle Thirties

170. Creamer; Sugar; Butter Dish; crystal, pink, late Thirties

171. LEAF Candy Dish, 6¼" with handle; same design in CLOVER shape, 6" including handle (not shown); pink, crystal, late Thirties, Federal Glass Co.

172. Dish, 6" square, pressed pattern, pink, crystal, late Thirties

216

173. MOONSTONE Tableware, Opalescent Hobnail, crystal with bluish-white, 1942-1946, Hocking Glass Co., pieces include: 10" Sandwich Plate; 7¾" Flat Bowl; 10 oz. Goblet; 3¼" Sugar and Creamer; 6" Clover Leaf Dish; 6½" Heart Bonbon; Cup and Saucer; 4¼" Candleholder; 6 oz. Sherbet; 6¼" Sherbet Plate; 5½" Dessert; 8" Luncheon; 7¾" Divided Relish Dish; 6½" Crimped Handled Bowl; 4¾" Puff Box and Cover; 5½" Vase; 6" Candy Jar and Cover; 9½" Crimped Bowl; 5½" Crimped Dessert (1942 listing)

174. FLORAGOLD Tableware, iridescent amber, crystal, early Fifties, Jeannette Glass Co. (included in response to inquiries), pieces available: 8½" Dinner Plate; 13½" Tray or Torte Plate; Cup and Saucer; 9½", 12" Scalloped Fruit Bowl; 5½" Scalloped Fruit Dish; 6" Round Butter Dish and Cover; ¼-lb. Covered Butter Dish (oblong); Salt and Pepper; 5¼" x 3½" Footed Nut or Candy Dish; Sugar and Cover and Creamer; 10 oz., 11 oz. Footed Tumbler; 64 oz. Water Pitcher; 6¾" Candy or Cheese Dish and Cover; 5½ oz. Low Footed Sherbet; 9½" Salad or Popcorn Bowl; 5½" Salad or Cereal Bowl; Two-light Candlestick; 4½" Fruit Dish; 8½" Fruit Bowl; 4⅛" Ash Tray or Coaster (1951 listing)

175. DOLPHIN Candy Jar and Cover, 8½" tall, opaque, jade green, early Thirties

176. Ice Bucket and Cover, 6" tall, jade green, middle Thirties

177. Plate, 7½", jade green, middle Thirties

178. LORAIN design, Sherbet, with laced-edge effect, milk white, Forties, Indiana Glass Co.

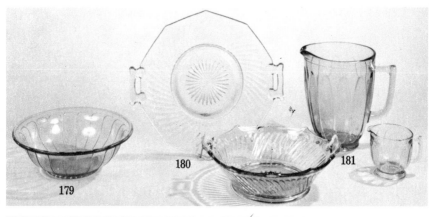

179. Bowl, 9", colonial style, green, early Thirties

180. TWISTED OPTIC Sandwich Tray, 11"; Handled Bowl, 9"; pink, green, crystal

181. Jug, 52 oz.; Creamer; green, early Thirties, Bartlett-Collins Co., additional pieces are: 8½" Plate; Cup and Saucer; Sherbet; Sugar; 5 oz., 9 oz., 12 oz. Tumbler; 14 oz. Footed Tumbler; 25 oz. Jug (in late Thirties made in opaque white and all-over enameled red, blue, yellow, and green)

182. Cream and Sugar, pink, blue-green, crystal, late Thirties, Indiana Glass Co., Line #624

183. Sandwich Plate, 10½"; Bowl, 8", handled; light green, light pink

184. MOROCCAN AMETHYST, made in early Sixties by Hazel-Ware, Continental Can Co. (included in response to many inquiries)

185. POPPY Vase, 8½", black satin finish (was also made in pink and green), early Thirties, United States Glass Co.

186. OCTAGON pattern tableware, 7½" Plate; Creamer; marked "U S G Co." (intertwined letters), black glass, early Thirties, United States Glass Co. (you will find additional pieces of this pattern)

220

187. OPTIC PANELED Candy Jar and Cover, 6"; Plate, 8"; Cone-shaped Sherbet; Round Sherbet; Cup and Saucer; green, late Twenties, marked ▽, Federal Glass Co. (you may find other pieces of this pattern)

188. Plate, 8", fine stippling, pink, green, amber

189. Grill Plate, 9½", green, amber, crystal, late Twenties, United States Glass Co.

190. Grill Plate, 10½", pink, green, early Thirties, United States Glass Co.

191. Goblet, 5½", stippling effect with flowers, dark green, late Twenties, Federal Glass Co.

192. Sherbet, "Federal Jr.", 4½ oz.; "Sr." 6 oz.; "Midget" 3½ oz.; pink, green, crystal, marked ▽, Federal Glass Co.

193. Cup and Saucer with fine stippling band (other pieces available in this pattern), pink, green, amber, late Twenties

194. BLOCK design, 10 oz. cup; 15 oz. Tumbler; medium heavy, medium-sized blocks, green, late Twenties

195. Square Jar and Cover, 4½"; Pitcher, 36 oz.; Bowl, 6", ruffled; Bowl and Cover, 6", round; pink, "Ultra-marine" (blue-green)

NOTE: *The following Items 196-204 are deep blue in color.*

196. Mixing Bowl, 7½"

197. Handled Plate, 6"

198. Nappy, 5¼"

199. Fine Ribbed Tumbler, 9 oz.

200. Sherbet, scalloped edge

201. Salt and Pepper, 2¾", marked ⋀, Thirties, Hazel Atlas Glass Co.

202. Pitchers, 3" and 4"

203. Jug, 80 oz., ice lipped, white sailboat motif

204. Cocktail Shaker, 10½", white decoration, has matching tumblers

205. RINGED TARGET Jug, 85 oz., ice lipped, pink

206. ROYAL pattern (once named "Windsor"), Jug, 85 oz. (also made in 64 oz. size); 5 oz., 9 oz., 12 oz. Tumblers; early and late Thirties, pink, green, crystal, red ("Royal Ruby"), Hocking Glass Co.

207. BIG BEN Tilt Jug, 85 oz. (also comes in 38 oz. size), pink, amber, crystal, late Thirties, Federal Glass Co.

208. PANEL style Jug, 65 oz., ice lipped, pink, amber, crystal, middle Thirties, Federal Glass Co.

209. PILLAR Optic (#1), Pitcher, 60 oz., pink, green, crystal, middle Thirties, Hocking Glass Co.

210. PILLAR OPTIC (#2), Pitcher, 80 oz., ice lipped, pink, green, crystal, middle Thirties, Hocking Glass Co.

211. DIAMOND line, 60 oz. Pitcher (also comes in 80 oz. size); 5 oz., 9 oz., 13 oz. Iced Tea Tumblers; pink, green, crystal, late Thirties, Anchor Hocking Glass Co.

212. Queen Anne Pitcher, 80 oz.; Tumblers, Footed, 15 oz. Iced Tea; pink, crystal, late Thirties, Anchor Hocking Glass Co.

213   214   215

216   217

218

213. Jug, 25 oz., early Thirties, Hazel Atlas Glass Co.

214. GEORGIAN pattern, Jug, 65 oz., ice lipped, (also comes in 9 oz. and 12 oz. tumblers), pink, green, amber, crystal, late Thirties, Federal Glass Co.

215. GEORGIAN line, Pitcher, 60 oz., ice lipped; Tumblers, 5 oz., 9 oz., 12 oz.; additional pieces are: 25 oz. Decanter with Crystal Stopper; 5½ oz. Sherbet; 6" Sherbet Plate; 2 oz. Whiskey; 7½ oz. Old Fashioned; pink, green, crystal, middle Thirties, Hocking Glass Co.

NOTE: Items 214 and 215 are not to be confused with the GEORGIAN pattern on page 92. All three names are, unfortunately, official ones.

216. CRISSCROSS pattern, 60 oz. Jug; 5 oz., 9 oz., 12 oz. Tumblers; green, crystal, early Thirties, Hocking Glass Co.

217. FINE RIBBED Tilt Jug, 42 oz., ice lipped, pink, deep blue, crystal (HOMESPUN Tilt Jug resembles this one)

218. CIRCLE design tableware, green, pink, crystal, late Twenties, early Thirties, available pieces include: 8" Plate; 10" Serving Plate; Cream and Sugar (same shape as 4" CAMEO); Cup; Saucer; Sherbet; 6" Sherbet Plate; 80 oz. Jug; 5 oz., 9 oz., 12 oz. Tumblers; 4 oz., 6 oz. Wine Goblets; Hocking Glass Co.

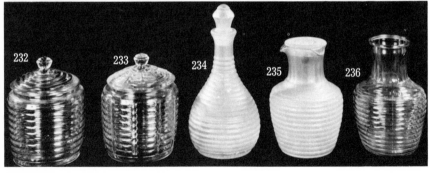

219. BLOCK Candy Dish, green satin finish, early Thirties, Hocking Glass Co.

220. Candlestick, 3'', pink satin finish, pink, green, crystal

221. MAYFAIR Cream and Sugar, pink satin finish, decorated, middle Thirties, Hocking Glass Co.

222. LACE EDGE Candlestick, pink satin finish, orchid decoration, middle Thirties, Hocking Glass Co.

223. PRINCESS Cream and Sugar, pink satin finish, green satin finish, floral decoration, early Thirties, Hocking Glass Co.

224. LACE EDGE Nappy, pink satin finish, middle Thirties, Hocking Glass Co.

225. Flower Block, 2½'' x 5½'', pink satin finish

226. ASTER Vase, 7½'' tall, white satin finish, late Twenties, United States Glass Co.

227. CAMEO Water Bottle and Stopper, 8½'', green satin finish, middle Thirties, Hocking Glass Co.

228. Vase, 9'', pink, red ("Royal Ruby"), crystal, late Thirties, Anchor Hocking Glass Co.

229. LACE EDGE Vase, 7'', pink satin finish, sometimes with orchid decoration, middle Thirties, Hocking Glass Co.

230. Vase, 5¼'', opaque white, Anchor Hocking Glass Co. (was advertised with OYSTER AND PEARLS pieces)

231. OYSTER AND PEARLS, 10½'' Console Bowl and 3½'' Candleholders; 5¼'' Heart-shaped Jelly Dish; white with "Dusty Rose" interior, white with "Springtime Green" interior, early Forties, Anchor Hocking Glass Co.

232. HORIZONTAL RIBBED Cookie Jar and Cover, ½ gal., pink, crystal, late Thirties, Anchor Hocking Glass Co.

233. PANELED AND RIBBED Cookie Jar and Cover, ½ gal., pink, crystal, late Thirties, Anchor Hocking Glass Co.

234. Decanter and Stopper, horizontal ribbed, 10½'' tall, green satin finish, green, dark green, crystal, middle Thirties, Hocking Glass Co.

235. Water Bottle and Cap, 54 oz., horizontal ribbed, green satin finish, "Frigidaire Ice Tea Server" inscribed on bottom, middle Thirties, Hocking Glass Co.

236. Water Bottle, without cap, green, crystal, late Thirties, Hocking Glass Co.

237. VITROCK Tableware, snowy white, 1935-1937, Hocking Glass Co., pieces include: 10" Dinner Plate; 4½" Cream Soup; 4" Dessert; Sugar; Creamer; Cup; Saucer; 9" Soup Plate; 8" Luncheon Plate; 7¼" Bread or Cream Soup; 6" Fruit Bowl; 7½" Cereal Bowl; 9½" Vegetable Bowl; 11½" Meat Platter

238. LAUREL Dinnerware (band of leaves and berries), marked "McK", comes in "French Ivory," "Jade Green," "Poudre Blue," and "White Opal," early Thirties, McKee Glass Co., pieces include: 9" Dinner Plate; 9" Grill Plate; 10¾" Oval Platter; 7½" Salad Plate; 4" Candlestick; 5" Fruit Dish; Footed Sherbet; Miniature Sugar and Creamer, 2"; #1 Sugar and Creamer; Cup and Saucer; additional pieces not shown are: 10½" Round Utility Bowl; 9" Soup Plate; Salt and Pepper; 6" Cereal Dish; 6" Bread and Butter Plate; Oval Vegetable Dish; 9" Round Vegetable Dish; 6" 3-toe Jelly; #2 Sugar Bowl and Creamer (low footed); 5" Oatmeal

239. Dinnerware, raised floral band, opaque ivory, opaque white, Butter Dish and Cover; Platter; Sugar and Creamer (you may find additional pieces to this pattern)

240. Bud Vase, 6", "Jadite," "Delfite," middle Thirties, Jeannette Glass Co.

241. SWIRL Plate, 9", "Delfite," middle Thirties, Jeannette Glass Co.

242. DORIC Sherbet, "Delfite," middle Thirties, Jeannette Glass Co.

243. Bowl, 9", "Poudre Blue," middle Thirties, McKee Glass Co., marked "McK"

244. Salt Shaker, 6", light blue opaque

245. Spoon Holder, jade green opaque

246. Ash Tray, "Jadite," "Delfite," middle Thirties, Jeannette Glass Co.

247. DORIC Nut or Candy Dish, 7", "Delfite," pink, green, middle Thirties, Jeannette Glass Co.

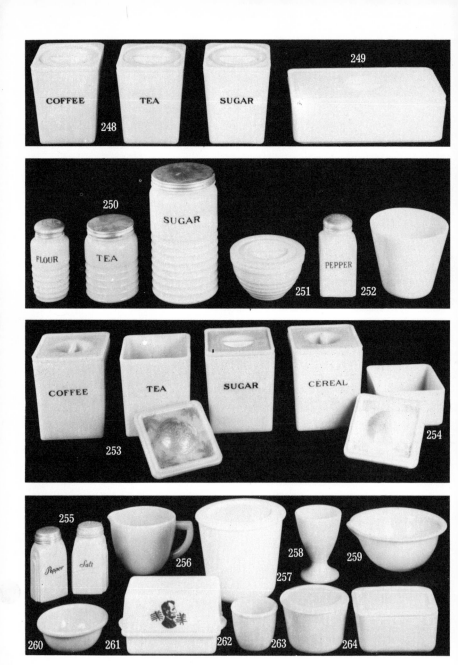

248. CEREAL SET: 4¼" x 4¼" (top measurement), 5" tall, Coffee; Tea; Sugar; Cereal; with covers

249. Refrigerator Tray and Cover, 4⅜" x 9¾" x 2⅝" high

250. CABINET SET: Flour (not shown are Sugar, Salt, Pepper), 4½"; Tea, 4½"; Sugar, 7½"; Dripping Bowl and Cover, 2½" x 4½"; all round

251. Pepper, 4¼", part of RANGE SET, square shapes (not shown are Salt, Sugar, and Flour)

252. Beater Bowl, 5" x 4½" tall

253. FLORAL CEREAL SET: floral design on underside of cover, 4¾" x 4¾" x 5¾" tall, Coffee; Tea; Sugar, Cereal; with covers

254. FLORAL Refrigerator Tray and Cover, 4¾" x 4¾" x 2¾" (floral design on underside of cover and on bottom)

NOTE: *Items 255-264 were made by McKee Glass Co. in the middle Thirties in "Jade Green," "French Ivory," and "White Opal," and all are marked "McK" on bottom.*

255. Salt and Pepper, 4¼", also in black glass

256. Measuring Cup, 16 oz.

257. Jar and Cover, 5¾" x 5" (cover measures 6¼")

258. Egg Cup, footed, 3¼" x 4¼" high

259. Mixing Bowl with pouring spout, 7"

260. Nappy, 4¼"

261. Butter Dish and Cover, 3" x 5½" (picture of Abe Lincoln on "White Opal")

262. Egg Cup, 2¾"

263. Round Jar and Cover, 4"

264. Square Jar and Cover, 4" x 5", marked "McK" on top of cover as well as on bottom of jar

265   266   267   268

269   270   271   272   273   274

275   276   277   278

279   280   281

265. Refrigerator Dish, 4" x 5" x 4" tall, light green opaque, with crystal cover

266. Reamer, used on measuring cup, green opaque

267. Reamer, "Jadite," "Delfite," middle Thirties, Jeannette Glass Co.

268. Reamer, "White Opal," middle Thirties, McKee Glass Co. (marked "McK")

269. Jar, round, 2", "Jadite," "Delfite," middle Thirties, Jeannette Glass Co.

270. RANGE SET: Sugar; Flour; Salt; Pepper; 4¾", opaque green (this set is a different shade of green and its pieces are a little larger than Item 251), middle Thirties, McKee Glass Co.

271. Measuring Pitcher, 6", ivory color

272. MEASURING CUP SET: 1 cup; ½ cup; ⅓ cup; ¼ cup; "Jadite," "Delfite," middle Thirties, Jeannette Glass Co.

273. Jug, 25 oz., milk white, marked ⒣ , Hazel Atlas Glass Co.

274. Egg Cup, opaque green

275. Mixing Bowl, 9", green, marked ⒣ , Hazel Atlas Glass Co., early Thirties

276. Mixing Bowl, 8½", pink, green, amber, crystal, Thirties, Federal Glass Co.

277. Salt and Pepper, 4", black glass, early Thirties, marked "McK", McKee Glass Co.

278. Mixing Bowls: 6½"; 7½"; 8½"; 9½"; 10½"; 11½"; pink, green, amber, "Vitrock" (snowy white), Thirties, Hocking Glass Co.

279. Salt and Pepper, 4"; 6"; part of a range set, dark green, early Thirties, Federal Glass Co.

280. CAMEO Vinegar Bottle, "Whitehouse Vinegar" inscribed on bottom, dark green (style and shape slightly different from CAMEO Water Bottle)

281. PROVISION JAR and Cover, 1 qt., green, crystal, middle Thirties, Hocking Glass Co.

234

282. Reamer, 7" x 2½" tall, pink, green, crystal, Indiana Glass Co.
283. Reamer, 5", pink, green, crystal, middle Thirties
284. Reamer, 4", fits on measuring cup, pink, green, middle Thirties
285. Reamer, 5½", pink, green, crystal, middle Thirties
286. Percolator Top, 2⅛", green, crystal, late Twenties, Thirties, Hocking Glass Co.
287. Butter Dish and Cover, 3" x 6" x 2" high, pink, green, crystal (you may find other pieces in this pattern)
288. Refrigerator Jar and Cover, vegetable motif, 4" x 4"; 4" x 8"; 8" x 8"; pink, green, amber, crystal, middle Thirties, Federal Glass Co. (also made in colors with no vegetable on cover)
289. Refrigerator Jar and Cover, square 5" x 5", green, crystal, middle Thirties, Hocking Glass Co.
290. Shaker, 4"; Bowl, 4"; pink, green, crystal
291. Syrup Pitcher, 4¼", pink, green, crystal, early Thirties
292. Kitchen Shakers: Spice; Sugar; Salt; Pepper; 5", green, early Thirties, Hocking Glass Co. (also available to match is a PANTRY SET, knobbed covers: Coffee; Sugar; Cereal; Flour; One Gallon Cookie Jar, square, enameled screw cover; Dripping Jar and Cover, 20 oz.)
293. Syrup Pitcher, 9 oz., green, crystal, Hocking Glass Co.
294. Syrup Pitcher, 6", green
295. Pepper Shaker, 4½", pink, green, early Thirties
296. Utility Pitcher, 16 oz., green, Thirties
297. Measuring Pitcher, 2 qt., green
298. Measuring Cup, 8 oz., pink, green, amber, crystal, middle Thirties, Federal Glass Co. (other companies made the same style), has "Kelloggs" inscribed on bottom
299. Measuring Cup, 8 oz., closed handle, pink, early Thirties
300. Measuring Jar, 16 oz., green, "Vidrio Products Corp. Chicago, Ill." inscribed on bottom
301. DONKEY POWDER JAR and Cover; POODLE POWDER JAR and Cover; pink, crystal, iridescent (elephant, deer, cat also made), late Thirties, Jeannette Glass Co.
302. Wine Goblet, 3", pink, crystal
303. Ash Tray, 5", green
304. Candy Jar and Cover, 4½", pink, green, middle Thirties
305. Dog Ash Tray (also elephant), pink, green, crystal, middle Thirties
306. Boot, 2", pink, green, Thirties
307. Ash Tray, 2-part, pink
308. Powder Dish and Cover, 4", pink, green, early Thirties
309. Ash Tray, 3", diamond design, center matchbox holder, green, early Thirties
310. Tumbler, bluish-green, part of child's set, Akro Agate Co.

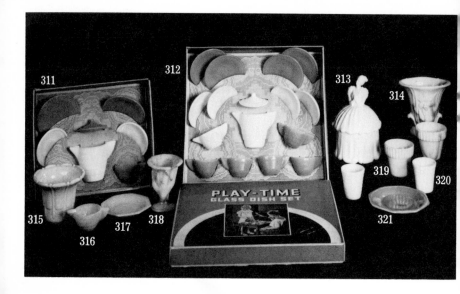

NOTE: *Items 311-321 were made by the Akro Agate Co.*

311. 8-Piece set: 2 Plates, 3¼"; 2 Cups; 2 Saucers; Teapot and Cover; opaque green, opaque white

312. 16-piece Set; 4 Plates, 3¼"; 4 Cups; 4 Saucers; Cream; Sugar; Teapot and Cover; green, white, blue

313. Powder Box and Cover, girl figure, pink, 6¼" tall, probably made in other colors

314. Vase, 4⅜"

315. Vase, 3"

316. Creamer, part of child's set, yellow

317. Plate, 3⅜", octagon-shaped, part of child's set

318. Vase, 3", hand design

319. Flower Pots: 2⅜"; 2¼"

320. Tumblers, 2 oz.

321. Plate, 4¼", octagon-shaped

Index

Trademarks of the Glass Companies

 Akro Agate Co.

 Anchor Hocking Corp.

 Bartlett-Collins Co.

 Cambridge Glass Co.

 Corning Glass Works
Macbeth-Evans Glass Co.

 Federal Glass Co.

 Hazel Atlas Glass Co.

 Heisey Glass Co.

 Hocking Glass Co.

 Indiana Glass Co.

 Jeannette Glass Co.

 McKee Glass Co.

 United States Glass Co.

 Westmoreland Glass Co.

From me to you

Most of you know me by now. You know me through your reading of these pages; we have met, and we are friends. We share more than a common interest: we share a great one. Through our efforts, Depression-era glassware will maintain its own place in the history of American glass. This is as it should be.

Truly, I am glad to have shared in this noble effort with you.